**Includes
one CD**

CHOCOLATE PATHWAY TO THE GODS

A diving god with a cacao pod offering,
accompanied by maize motifs. (Postclassic
Maya painted vase from a region near
Tulum, Mexico)

MEREDITH L. DREISS *and* SHARON EDGAR GREENHILL

CHOCOLATE

PATHWAY TO THE GODS

THE UNIVERSITY OF ARIZONA PRESS   *Tucson*

The University of Arizona Press

© 2008 Meredith L. Dreiss and Sharon Edgar Greenhill

All rights reserved

www.uapress.arizona.edu

Library of Congress Cataloging-in-Publication Data appear on the last printed page of this book.

Manufactured in China on acid-free, archival-quality paper.

13 12 11 10 09 08   6 5 4 3 2 1

A squirrel eating a cacao pod.
(Maya ceramic whistle)

A female figure embellished with cacao beans on her torso and arms. She emerges from a conical lid covered in cacao beans, holding a vessel containing two cacao pods. (Classic period censer, Southern coast, Guatemala, Museo Nacional de Arqueología y Etnología, Guatemala; photograph by Jorge Pérez de Lara)

contents

~~~~~~~~~

Split cacao pods, exposing pulp and embedded cacao beans. (Tabasco, Mexico; photograph by George O. Jackson Jr.)

preface and Acknowledgments

The idea for this book was inspired by photographs I saw in 1986 of an exquisitely shaped interlocking chocolate vessel recovered from Tomb 19 at the archaeological site of Río Azul, Guatemala. Being a confirmed chocoholic, I decided that everyone, not just archaeologists, should know about chocolate's fascinating 3,500-year history in ancient Mesoamerica. When I mentioned the concept to my brother, documentary filmmaker Grant Mitchell, he said, "Forget the book, let's do a film."

When the film project evolved into reality a decade later, I hired coauthor and coproducer Sharon Edgar Greenhill to help with every aspect of the process, and together we spent years tracking down images and modern-day stories for our film, *Chocolate: Pathway to the Gods*. This book, with the same title, grew out of that original effort.

Most of our research on chocolate and the cacao tree, from which chocolate is derived, has been centered in the Maya area of Mesoamerica, specifically the ancient cacao-growing regions of Mexico, Belize, Honduras, and Guatemala. We have also drawn information from the Oaxaca Valley and the Valley of Mexico, where all things chocolate were (and still are) elevated to sacred importance. Although the cacao tree grew wild in the lower Amazon and in the foothills of the Venezuelan and Colombian Andes, there is scant evidence for ancient cultivation and ritualized uses of chocolate in these regions of South America. Instead, the indigenous people of Mesoamerica were the first to cultivate and transform cacao beans (seeds) into the heavenly, aromatic concoction we know today as chocolate, a sacred delicacy highly prized by gods, kings, and merchants in pre-Columbian times.

In the course of our investigations, we have examined numerous ethnographic, archaeological, linguistic, historical, and botanical documents. Many images come from rare surviving codices and books, pre-Columbian objects, private photographic collections, and digital images from our filming expeditions. Likewise, our text is based on layers of interpretations by the best researchers in the field, as well as from unlikely informants whom we encountered along the way.

Our research has taught me more about Maya culture, art, and archaeology than I ever thought possible, and this is because we wove the subject together from many different points of view. I want to especially thank my coauthor, Sharon Edgar Greenhill, whose artistic eye and creativity helped me to see way beyond the horizon of archaeological data and then helped me to write about these findings. Without her, this book would not have been possible.   *Meredith L. Dreiss*

When archaeologist Meredith Dreiss first solicited my help in March 1998 to produce a documentary film about chocolate, my initial exhilaration quickly turned to panic. I had just completed an architectural and historic documentation of an obscure form of sixteenth-century architecture that dotted the landscape of Michoacan, Mexico. How could I contribute to a subject so steeped in a pre-Columbian soup that it seemed far beyond my area of knowledge and expertise? Besides, as someone who habitually avoided commercial sweets, could I put heart and soul into such a project when my only exposure to chocolate had been to a product adulterated with sugar and other commercial additives, such as soy lecithin, corn syrup, and gluten, which dilute chocolate's nutritional value? The rich trove of artistic and iconographic treasures we uncovered during those first few months of research quickly underscored why I had immersed myself into a Mesoamerican world years earlier: it is a place where human, natural, and supernatural forces are intricately and irrevocably intertwined, and here was a food whose iconography confirmed it.

The visual legacies of cacao, the cacao tree, and chocolate resurface over and over, whether as a painted element executed on a Maya ceramic cup by a diligent scribe, as an architectural embellishment on a Yucatan temple capstone, as a cartoonlike image jumping from the *amate* pages of Mixtec and Maya codices, or as a three-dimensional molded clay figure laden with cacao pods. What were these images telling us? By stringing that legacy together over a continuum of time and space, we sought to unveil the complex symbolism that chocolate exuded within a ritual ancient Mesoamerica, while exposing comparable antecedents throughout contemporary Mexico and Central America.

We became intoxicated by the vibrant images of ceramics, figures, murals, carvings, monuments, and codices from this ancient world—over 150, to be exact. But as our filmmaker, Grant Mitchell, had warned us, we had far too many still images for a media based on motion. As the image bank grew, the project seemed too massive an undertaking. Our film was completed in 2005, but at a heartbreaking price: most of our treasure of extraordinary still images had to be cut. These images, along with several clips from the film, form the corpus of this book.

As a result of this project and Meredith's persistent vision, I have tasted chocolate so pure and devoid of sugar and milk additives that I now understand why it was the food of the gods and gave warriors energy. In sampling ancient formulas, I was so startled by my first sensory hit of capsicum released from unadulterated chocolate infused with red chili pepper that I was unable to contain the "Wow!" that rolled off my lips. And I marvel at how the sacred cacao tree and its precious gift of chocolate resonate today as mnemonic symbols, still pulling the heart and soul of a Mesoamerican world along a continuum of time, space, and ritual. *Sharon Edgar Greenhill*

Acknowledgments

We give special thanks to Grant and Tiziana Mitchell, Cynthia and George Mitchell, George O. Jackson Jr., Allen Young, Frederick Bove, Elaine Gonzales, Keith Prufer, Patricia McAnany, Polly Peterson, Karen Dakin, Vicente Cacep, Justin Kerr, John Pohl, Bruce Love, Mary Miller, Simon Martin, Barbara MacLeod, Robert Sharer, Jeanette Favrot Peterson, Oswaldo Chinchilla Mazariegos with Museo Popol Vuh, Mimi Crossley, Grant Hall, Steve Black, Terry Powis, Thomas R. Hester, Fred Valdez, David O. Brown, Christina Luke, Payson Sheets, Michael Hironymous with Rare Books and Manuscripts at the University of Texas Benson Latin American Collection, Jeffrey Hurst, Sulvano Sho of Belize, Edwin Barnhart, Marion Popenoe Hatch, Janet Berlo, Janine Gasco, Richard Haley, the late Luis Luján Múñoz, Carlos Barrios and family of Guatemala City, Maria Elena "Nana" Winter and family of Coban in Guatemala, the Caal family members of Coban, Ana Urizar, Judith Strupp Green, Francesca Isabel Padilla Arévolo of Comalcalco, Tabasco, and the Fuentes family of Mexico City.

We are grateful for the support of family members Adrienne Dreiss, Emily Greenhill Pierce and Adam Pierce, and Jeff Sikora, as well as the staff at the University of Arizona Press, confirmed chocoholics, who believed in us from the beginning. We would especially like to acknowledge archaeologist Dana Anthony, whose editorial acumen finally shook this book off the drafting table and on to our publishers.

An Aztec male figure holding a cacao pod. (Stone Sculpture, no provenance; photograph by Sr. Carlos Varillas; Courtesy of Fundacion Amparo/Museo Amparo)

CHOCOLATE   PATHWAY TO THE GODS

introduction

〜〜〜〜〜〜〜〜〜〜〜

And those who had taken part in the war returned home in order, singing and dancing and bringing with them those who were to be sacrificed, decorated with feathers and jade on their wrists and ankles, and with strings of cacao beans around their necks.   *Garcia de Palacio, 1576*

Why was a treat such as chocolate hanging around the necks of sacrificial victims, one might ask? Garcia de Palacio's eyewitness account of chocolate's role in a gruesome human sacrifice—represented by the necklace of cacao beans—may jar our modern sensibilities. But the obsession with chocolate has not always been driven purely by sensory pleasure. The passion for many foods throughout the world is rooted in ancient rituals that appeased the gods, and this is certainly the case for chocolate and the chocolate-giving cacao tree.

The place held by chocolate in matters of creation, fertility, death, and rebirth is just now being understood after years of scholarly focus on maize (corn) as the primary sacred food of pre-Columbian Mesoamericans. In this book, we reveal how chocolate, like maize, became linked to some of the most fundamental of Mesoamerican rites in both ancient and modern times. While we have relied somewhat on colonial accounts and contemporary research to tell our story, we primarily depend on pre-Columbian art, mythology, and glyphic texts to unveil the multilayered complexity of ritual and chocolate in Mesoamerican cosmology.

Mesoamerica is a contiguous cultural area encompassing portions of Mexico, Belize, Guatemala, Honduras, El Salvador,

Figure I.1   A sacrificial victim with a cacao pod necklace. (Late Classic Maya ceramic whistle)

Nicaragua, and Costa Rica. Although botanical evidence suggests that the cacao tree may have originated in South America, the indigenous peoples of Mesoamerica were the ones to hold the cacao tree in greatest esteem. For not only did its branches and trunk bear pods from which the seeds were extracted, to be processed into sumptuous chocolate, but it also appears to have been endowed with the cosmic powers of the World Tree that enabled a dialogue between humans and the supernaturals.

Stunning iconography from Olmec, Maya, Zapotec, Mixtec, and Aztec art lead us to this and other conclusions about cacao. Cacao images and glyphic texts not only cover the surfaces of ancient ceramics, stone monuments, painted murals, and architectural elements but also appear on the bark or deerskin pages of the folding-screen books, or "codices," produced by the pre-Columbian and colonial-era Mesoamericans. The multifarious themes include cacao gods and goddesses; elites with chocolate drinks and cacao pods; divination rituals using cacao; ballplayers with cacao motifs; promiscuous monkeys holding cacao pods; sacrificed jaguars covered in cacao; cacao pods representing extracted hearts; heads and bodies emerging from cacao trees; and cacao pods with anthropomorphic faces. Some of these themes are set within a sacred landscape of caves, cenotes (sinkholes), mountains, and other natural elements.

The eighteenth-century naturalist Carolus Linnaeus gave the "chocolate tree" its scientific name: *Theobroma cacao,* or "Food of the Gods"—and for good reason. The cacao tree emerges from creation mythology as a sacred World Tree, worthy of the protection of cacao gods and goddesses. As a symbol of abundance, rulership, and ancestry, the cacao tree serves as a metaphorical conduit by which human souls and gods travel between Earth, Sky, and Underworld. Indeed, cacao is pictured in codices and on ceramic vases as offerings by deities in ritual ceremonies and sacrifices.

Humans replicated these divine activities in their own offerings of cacao and chocolate to the gods and to each other. Cacao played a major role in maintaining the life cycles of birth, death, and rebirth on earth. In addition, cacao is related to the underworld domain of caves, as a part of the sacred landscape. At the archaeological sites of El Tajin, El Baúl, and Bilbao, the juxtaposition of cacao, jaguars, and ballplayers on stone monuments poses intriguing questions about cacao's role in the mythological ballgame. And in cacao-growing regions, we find agricultural festivals dedicated to cacao, as an offering to both ancient deities and Catholic saints. Although to this day cacao and chocolate are integrated into major events such as marriages, baptisms, and funerals, nothing in modern life compares to the cacao pod's symbolic association with the extraction of the human heart during sacrifice!

Figure I.2
*A cacao tree
of the* forastero
*variety in
Tabasco, Mexico.*

Cacao may have been essential to the cosmic soul of the Mesoamerican world, but its economic value was the true source of power, greed, and domination. Architectural capstones from Maya ruins depict cacao associated with the Maya god of abundance and wealth, perhaps reflecting the restriction of the chocolate drink to the elites. The lure of this highly prized commodity catalyzed an extensive trade industry throughout Mesoamerica, creating a powerful merchant class with patron gods and provoking fourteenth-century Aztec domination of the cacao-growing regions in Mexico and Central America. As the "happy money" that grew on trees, the cacao bean was the medium of exchange for every sort of commodity imaginable; as with any form of currency, it was often counterfeited. When the bedazzled European conquerors in the sixteenth century appropriated this once-sacred cacao tree for their own gains, they forever changed the world of chocolate.

However, the seduction of cacao has always resided in its consumption. Modern chemical analyses of pre-Columbian ceramics prove that Mesoamericans have been eating and drinking chocolate since at least 1500 BC. Vessels, bowls, and platters that were specifically manufactured for ritual cacao dishes and chocolate drinks have evolved in form over thousands of years. Glyphic texts appearing by 400 AD on these ceramics give us clues as to the actual chocolate drink recipes, most of which are still enjoyed today. But an intriguing question arises from our research: why was the foam on top of the chocolate drink so revered?

Early Mesoamericans were not only enamored with the taste of this drink but also understood that it was good for body and soul. Chocolate has been one of the world's favorite curatives and stimulants throughout time. Long hailed as an aphrodisiac, chocolate has an allure that has created a cascade of myths about this "food of the devil" and matters of the heart. As it turns out, there *is* a connection to the heart: modern chemical analyses have isolated the heart-saving antioxidants within dark chocolate, confirming what the ancients knew intuitively.

The mythohistories that cast cacao and chocolate within a supernatural world carry through to the modern-day issues of rainforest ecology of cacao cultivation within Central America and Mexico. An example of ecological biodiversity, the botanical variances of cacao were often portrayed in Maya iconography. Multifarious plant, animal, and insect life both benefited from and nurtured cacao, but large-scale modern cultivation has departed from that balance with pesticides, clear-cutting, and monocultural plantings. The gods, while unaware of the term *biodiversity,* certainly understood how to balance their universe with chocolate.

A Note on Terminology

The word *cacao,* especially as it appears in chapters 1 and 2, is used as a general term applied to the chocolate drink, balls of chocolate, and the seeds and pod—all derived from the cacao tree. Within many Maya dialects spoken throughout Mexico and Central America, the term *cacao* (or *kakaw*) is often interchangeable with the word *chocolate* as we know it today. It is not to be confused with the word *cocoa,* the modern-day version of powered chocolate combined with milk solids. Nor is it the same as *coca,* the Andean plant from which the drug cocaine is extracted.

We use the term *iconography* to describe the images painted and carved on pre-Columbian artifacts, architecture, and documents. Symbolic meanings are attached to these images that, when first created, conveyed messages as conventional to ancient readers as the arches of McDonald's are to us today. So as we look at the personages, deities, elements of nature, and mysterious cosmological or supernatural events that appear with cacao and chocolate, a keen eye within a multidisciplinary approach is needed to make sense of the complex layers of pictorial metaphors. We have relied on the many keen eyes of researchers before us, whose insights have sharpened our eyes. Likewise, in drawing a textual message from the hieroglyphics that often accompany these images, we have consulted the work of those who have persistently deciphered the hieroglyphics over many decades. In the end, this iconographic story is our way of reinterpreting today's world through the ancient Mesoamerican portal of cacao and chocolate.

chocolate and the supernatural realm: food of the gods

Kakaw ujanal, cacao is his food.   *Dresden Codex*

Our story of chocolate and the sacred cacao tree begins in a primeval, supernatural world of Mesoamerican mythology. Creator gods, benevolent and not-so-benevolent forces, and superheroes of cosmic proportions played out dramas of life, death, and rebirth in search of cosmic and ecological order against a backdrop of Maya, Mixtec, and Aztec stories. The four corners of the world were set, the sky was raised from the face of the earth with a central World Tree, and humanity was created during the course of these dramas.

Chocolate and the cacao tree, along with its pods and seeds, play a pivotal role in these stories. Cacao appears as one of the first foods, as a sacred tree, and as an offering between the gods. These metaphorical representations suggest that cacao was a coveted item among supernatural beings, so special that it existed in a mythological time before creation, and that its role as a negotiating tool ensured the balance and order of the Underworld, Earth, and Sky.

The Maya god Chac, whose food is cacao, borne by the Opossum God. (Dresden Codex)

cacao woman: fertility goddess from the dawn of creation

One of our first clues that the supernaturals required chocolate and cacao comes from the Popol Vuh, the Quiché Maya's sixteenth-century book of creation, which recounts from even-more-ancient sources the setting up of the world. The Popol Vuh opens its poetic narrative by remembering how things were in the predawn time

Figure 1.1   A cacao goddess. (Late Classic
Maya ceramic figurine)

before creation. Only the sky, sea, and an earth whose face was still unrecognizable
existed: "This is the beginning of the Ancient Word, here in this place called *Quiché*.
. . . Now it still ripples, now it still murmurs, ripples, it still sighs, still hums, and it
is empty under the sky. . . . There is not yet one person, one animal, bird, fish, crab,
tree, rock hollow, canyon, meadow, forest."[1] But there are deities, powerful creator
deities, including "the Maker, Modeler, named Bearer, Begetter, Hunahpú Possum,
Hunahpú Coyote, Great White Peccary, Coati, Sovereign Plumed Serpent."[2] And

Chapter One

Figure 1.2   A cacao goddess with a vessel on her head. (Late Classic Maya ceramic figurine)

there is food—corn, cacao, and other staples—as well as a goddess or guardian of cacao, Cacao Woman. She is called forth by Blood Moon (the moon goddess and the soon-to-be mother of the mythical Hero Twins, Hunahpú and Xbalanque) in a frantic search for food so that Blood Moon would not be killed: "Come on out, rise up now, come on out, stand up now: Thunder Woman, Yellow Woman, Cacao Woman and Cornmeal Woman."[3]

Cacao, like corn, appears to have been an important staple for the gods and other early mythical personas; it required the protection of a multifaceted fertility goddess. Late Classic period clay figurines retrieved from western Guatemala, a region once dominated by intense cacao production, recall such a female deity (figs. 1.1 and 1.2). These effigies are laden with cacao pods growing directly out of their bodies, mimicking the way cacao grows from tree trunks. They have facial features identifying them as supernaturals: tattoolike markings on the jaw and a filed *tau* (T-shaped) tooth. Their eyes are open, indicating that they are alive, not dead. Some of the Cacao Woman figurines have two small baby effigies on the back, one hanging from each shoulder, while others haul pots, possibly for chocolate, on either the head or the back. The uniformity of these ceramic figurines suggests an important personage, a goddess perhaps, of abundance or fertility.

was there a cacao god?

In addition, there might have been a masculine counterpart to Cacao Woman.[4] The youthful cacao god in figure 1.3, likewise from the Pacific coastal region, sprouts cacao pods from his body, again in much the same way as a cacao tree. Another youthful god with cacao pods growing from his body appears on the unique stone bowl in figure 1.4. The shape and size of this carved vessel replicate the common calabash-gourd cup typically used for drinking chocolate since ancient times. The portrayed deity is incised in three cartouches, two of which are still identifiable. In addition to the cacao pods growing from his body, corn tassels grow from his elongated head, a feature of the tonsured maize god. In the main cartouche, he sits on a thronelike mat and points to a vase with an incised glyph on the front. On the second cartouche, he is floating or flying, while writing on (or pointing at) what appears to be a codex. Supernaturals are often depicted writing in codices or painting ceramics, symbolic of a creation act. A water bird flies above and a ruler's mat appears below. Some of the glyphic inscriptions translate as "youthful sky person." If not a young cacao god, he could represent a dual aspect of a cacao-corn deity.

Figure 1.3   A young cacao god. (Late Classic Maya ceramic figurine)

The Late Classic period effigy in figure 1.5 of an old man sprouting cacao pods may represent an old cacao god. His crossed arms recalls a style found in the Cotzumalhuapa area of Esquintla in southwestern Guatemala, the heart of an ancient cacao-growing region.[5] From the site of El Baúl in this same region, another deified image carved into a stone monument wears an enormous headdress decorated with a cacao pod and leaves. For generations, local Guatemalans have referred to this imposing figure as the god of cacao (fig. 1.6).[6]

A ceramic figure of a seated male deity from the Classic period may also be a cacao god (see fig. 6.13). A cut-open cacao pod attached to an umbilical cord snakes from the top of his loincloth, as if emerging from his navel. He has the deified markings of a tau tooth, and remnants of white paint, perhaps representing the froth of chocolate, surround his mouth. In Mesoamerican symbolism, the navel is a metaphorical portal to the Otherworld, center of the universe, where the World Tree originates.

The concept of a cacao god may have reached beyond the geographic region of the Maya culture. On a page from the Codex Nuttall, a pre-Columbian Mixtec dynastic history dating as far back as AD 692, Lord Seven Crocodile holds up a small, offertory effigy. He, too, like our earlier examples, sprouts cacao pods from his body (fig. 1.7).[7]

Figure 1.4 (opposite)   Cacao deity. Above: A youthful cacao/maize deity with cacao pods growing from his limbs. Below: The same deity floating or flying. (Front and reverse views of a Late Classic Maya stone bowl)

Figure 1.5   An old cacao god with pods growing from his body. (Late Classic Maya ceramic figurine from the Cotzumalhuapa area, Esquintla, Guatemala)

Figure 1.6   A cacao deity wearing a headdress of cacao leaves and a cacao pod. (Late Classic Maya stone monument from El Baúl, Cotzumalhuapa area, Esquintla, Guatemala)

Figure 1.7   Lord Seven Crocodile holds up an idol with cacao pods growing from its body. (Codex Nuttall)

Was cacao used to Make Humans?

The Popol Vuh strongly suggests that cacao was one of the ingredients used to create humankind. After several failed attempts with wood, mud, and other compounds, the creator gods finally found the right substances to form an acceptable human being: the foodstuffs within the clefted mountain called "Split Place" or "Mountain of Sustenance."[8] It was a place filled with a variety of foods including "sweet things, thick with yellow corn, white corn, and thick with *pataxte* and cacao."[9] Despite the ambiguous nature of the Popol Vuh text, all of these foods, including cacao, appear to have formed the flesh and corpus of human beings.[10]

Images of split places where life begins appear throughout Olmec, Maya, Mixtec, and Aztec iconography, such as on the Early Classic painted, stuccoed vase in figure 1.8. Here, a stylized cacao tree, topped by a bird, emerges from a "split place" mountain, reinforcing cacao's link to one of the most sacred landscape features of pre-Columbian creation stories: the cave within a mountain. When gods choose to reveal themselves, they emerge from the open maw of the earth, or caves, that give access to the Underworld. Through these same portals, humans travel to where the gods live, whether to pay homage, ask for favors, or have a dialogue with them.

Figure 1.8 (opposite)   A quetzal bird resting in a cacao tree that is emerging from a "split place" mountain. The blowgunner appears at the left edge of the image. Comb and bar signs resembling the Maya fire glyph appear along the lower band. (Classic painted stucco, tripod vase)

Figure 1.9 (above)   Monkeys, squirrels, and human limbs intertwined with cacao pods. (Late Classic Maya vase)

Figure 1.10 (below)   A monkey and hunters with a deer sacrifice in front of a stylized cacao tree. (Maya vase)

monkeys and cacao

The long-limbed spider monkey and the vocal howler monkey are frequently illustrated together with cacao. In the natural world, these wily creatures thrive in the same tropical environment as cacao, frolicking among the cacao branches while splitting open the hard pods to eat the white, tasty pulp surrounding the cacao beans and, thus, dispersing the seeds for future growth (fig. 1.9). On a molded vase from Early Classic Guatemala (fig. 1.10), an animated monkey appears to be orchestrating the activity as a bearded man sacrifices a deer in front of a cacao tree. In the same scene, a blowgunner wearing a headband and having what could be cacao pods growing outward from his feet takes aim at a bird atop the cacao tree. The headband on one and the beard on the other suggest that they are the mythical Hero Twins.

Figure 1.11   A monkey "companion spirit" holding a cacao pod. (Late Classic Maya cylindrical vase)

In creation stories, monkeys appear both as ancestors to humans associated with an older period of chaos and as supernatural beings. In the Popol Vuh, for instance, when the creator gods became annoyed with and disappointed in the unresponsive humans they had formed from wood during the second creation period, the gods turned them into chattering, mischievous monkeys who were forever destined to swing from trees.[11] In Aztec mythology, they were also human ancestors and survivors of the second creation era under the rule of Quetzalcoatl, the great creator god.[12] Noted Mayanist Linda Schele has suggested that monkeys were spirited transformers who created chaos by tearing apart the old world in preparation for its re-creation and thus helped with the transition from the previous creation into this one.[13] On the vase in figure 1.11, a supernatural howler monkey (who may be a *way* or *wayab'*, that is, a co-essence, an animal spirit) holds a cacao pod as he walks in procession with the Waterlily Jaguar and the flesh version of the death god, who carries an olla (jar).

As supernatural beings, monkeys assumed the role of patron of writing and the arts, and monkey-men are depicted as scribes and as dancers. The most renowned monkey-men, Hun B'atz (One Monkey) and Hun Chouén (One Artisan), appear in the Popol Vuh epic as the half-brothers of the Hero Twins who were turned into monkeys as punishment for their malevolent deeds.[14] Banished to the yellow *canté* tree, they were destined to serve the Hero Twins much in the same manner that the canté tree (*Gliricidia sepium*), referred to as *madre de cacao,* serves the cacao tree with its shade.[15]

The sacred tree: conduit to other realms

Trees, like many other elements of the natural world, are important cosmic metaphors on many different levels. Throughout Mesoamerican creation stories, the World Tree or First Tree, the axis mundi, is the center of the universe and a primordial source of all life. Mimicking the botanical realities of a tree, with roots secured in the ground and branches reaching toward the sky, the World Tree connects the vertical realms of Sky, Earth, and Underworld. The celestial realm could encompass as many as thirteen layers; the Underworld, as many as nine. In some Maya creation myths, the World Tree holds the Sky up from the Earth. One of its Maya names, Wakah Chan ("raised-up sky"), emphasizes this phenomenon.[16] Linda Schele and archaeologist David Freidel have suggested that the World Tree appeared to the ancient Maya arched across the sky as the Milky Way.[17] As symbols of abundance, rulership, and ancestry, trees were conduits for departed souls and gods to travel between all three realms.[18]

Which tree became a World Tree seems to have depended on its ubiquity within a given region. Throughout much of Maya art, the World Tree was depicted as the native ceiba, or giant silk-cotton tree (*Ceiba pentandra*), with its spike-laden trunk. In central Mexico, it was represented by the *ahuehuete,* or Moctezuma cypress tree (*Taxodium mucronatum*), which is native to Mexico.[19] But in important cacao-growing regions of Central America, the World Tree was sometimes the cacao tree (see fig. 6.4 for a possible example).

Offering vessels, or censers (*incensarios*), were metaphoric portals associated with the center of the universe connecting Earth and Sky and thus symbolically functioned as a World Tree. The rising smoke from burning copal inside the censer served as an intermediary between the human world and the divine. This smoke is often depicted in Classic period Maya iconography as plantlike volutes.[20] At Copan, a Maya site in

Figure 1.12   A Late Classic Maya censer with cacao pods from Copan in Honduras.

cacao-rich Honduras, unearthed censers are often covered with the spikes of the ceiba and thus, by association, the axis mundi.[21] However, many of them are also covered with cacao pods. The censer in figure 1.12, now housed in the Peabody Museum of Archaeology and Ethnology, has cacao pods around the top of its base and a five-petal cacao flower on top of its lid.

Sacred trees also were portrayed as directional trees that delineated the cardinal directions of north, south, east, and west. They appear as such in cosmic diagrams in

Postclassic Maya and Aztec codices, as well as in native-written colonial texts.[22] These diagrams all share one thing in common: they illustrate the union of time and space by charting the daily course of the sun spatially through time, often utilizing trees drawn at the four cardinal directions to make this distinction clear.

An Aztec diagram in the Codex Féjérvary-Mayer (fig. 1.13) is of particular interest because it places the cacao tree as the cardinal directional tree to the south within a schematic four-sided cosmos. As in most Mesoamerican directional diagrams, it places the east direction at the top of the image, the west at the bottom. As the directional tree to the south, this cacao tree denotes the Land of the Dead and the Underworld. It is flanked on the right by the Aztec maize god, Cinteotl, and by the Aztec death god, Mictlantecuhtli, on the left.[23] The tree emerges from what may be the jaws of the Underworld serpent, a theme often duplicated in Maya imagery. The bird on top, in this case a parrot, identifies the cacao tree as a World Tree.

Trees were also natural metaphors of ancestral "family trees" among ruler lineages. Images of deities being "born" out of trees or transforming into trees appear throughout Mesoamerican art. The concept of ancestral trees most likely originated with Mesoamerica's first great civilization, the Olmecs, which reached its apogee before the time of Christ in the humid lowlands of Mexico's Gulf Coast.

Evidence that the cacao tree served as an ancestral tree is found on Classic period architectural and ceramic artifacts. At the monumental site of Chichen Itza in Yucatan, a region where cacao trees were cultivated in moist sinkholes (cenotes), two supportive, stone piers at the entrance of the Temple of the Owls are excellent examples of this phenomenon. The identical piers (fig. 1.14) have low relief images of a cacao tree carved on their north sides. Jade disks and cacao pods—both esteemed symbols of abundance and preciousness linked to life-giving properties—cover the trees.

Emerging from a hole at the base, each pier is the tenoned sculpture of a human figure with his arms crossed over the front of his chest. He is wearing a necklace and bracelets, and large volutes extend from his nostrils across his cheeks. On either side of his mouth are additional scrolls. The semicircle motif above the tenoned opening may be an umbilical cord of divine origin, as suggested by the presence of the feathered jade ornament across it. All of this seems to indicate that the human figure

Figure 1.13 (opposite)   An Aztec cosmic diagram
with the cacao tree as the directional tree to the
south (east is up). (Codex Féjérvary-Mayer)

Figure 1.14   An anthropomorphic figure emerging as a cacao tree covered with jade ornaments. (Late Classic Maya stone pier from Temple of the Owls, Chichen Itza)

emerging from the cacao tree is connected by his umbilical cord to the gods, symbolizing his right to rulership.[24]

In figure 1.15, a ceramic vase duplicates this event. Again, a figure with crossed arms over his chest emerges from the base of a cacao tree. The god K'awil (the embodiment of abundance, lineage, and rulership) sits with crossed legs to the left, gesturing toward the tree. A person just below K'awil is grinding what may be the seeds from the cacao pods into chocolate, perhaps intended for a ritual event, as tamales are also being prepared in this painted scene. Kneeling on the other side of the tamales is a man whose mouth is stained with chocolate. The narrative suggests that the right to rulership is being legitimized by the connection to this sacred cacao tree.

The cacao tree icon for "dynastic rights" appears on the tomb of at least one Maya ruler during the Classic period: Pakal the Great, seventh-century king of Palenque. Portraits of his ancestors, each emerging from a crack in the earth as a specific fruit tree, are carved on the four sides of the lid of his stone sarcophagus, which was found

Figure 1.15   A palace scene of an anthropomorphic figure emerging from a cacao tree. (Late Classic Maya cylindrical vase)

deep in his funerary temple (the Temple of the Inscriptions). One of his ancestors, his mother Lady Zac-Kuk, emerges as a cacao tree with cacao pods and flowers on both ends of the sarcophagus lid; she, not Pakal's father, was the one who carried the royal blood. Her portrayal as a cacao tree verified this lineage and, therefore, Pakal's legitimate claim to the throne (fig. 1.16).[25]

A right to rulership through lineage seems to be validated by stafflike cacao trees, such as in a scene incised on a jadeite plaque recovered from the cenote at Chichen Itza (fig. 1.17). Here, a lord clutches a cacao tree in the form of a staff. Circular jade pendants are along the right edge, perhaps as symbols of preciousness. In another instance found in the sixteenth-century Madrid Codex (fig. 1.18), the flower god, Ahaw Nik, sits between two small cacao trees while clutching one of them like a staff.[26]

The rollout photograph (a flattened image of a curved surface) of the Early Classic vase in figure 1.19 illustrates a mortuary scene in which the deceased is resurrected as a cacao tree. On the left side of this incised vessel, a dead man wrapped in a burial bundle lies on a bench while mourners, impersonating the maize god, lament his death. On the other side, the dead man (now reduced to bones) is being reborn as a cacao tree that sprouts up from the grave. On either side of him are other family members, perhaps his mother and father, resurrected as other types of fruit trees. His transformation as a cacao tree metaphorically completes the cycle of life, death, and rebirth.

Other examples of the transformative powers of the cacao tree originate from a story found in the Popol Vuh. It relates to One Hunahpú, known as the maize god, the father of the mythological Hero Twins. He, along with his twin brother, Seven Hunahpú, enter Xibalba, the Maya Underworld, and are defeated in a ballgame by One Death and Seven Death, Lords of the Underworld. They are sacrificed and buried at the Place of Ball Game Sacrifice. One Hunahpú's head is placed, according to the Popol Vuh, in the fork of a calabash tree that grows next to the ballgame court, and the head comes to life.[27]

However, the Maya vase featured in figure 1.20 suggests that in the Classic period, the tree of this mythical event could have been the cacao tree. The decapitated head of One Hunahpú hangs in the midst of cacao pods from the trunk of the tree, emerging as a pod with cacao flowers surrounding it. The two trees on the vase are framed by two seated figures, perhaps the Hero Twins, one of whom talks with a waterbird. In the upper branch of one of the cacao trees, a cacao pod with facial features suggests the transformation of One Hunahpú into a cacao pod (or vice versa).

Indeed, the cacao tree may have been more prominently featured in Classic

Figure 1.16   Lady Zac-Kuk, mother of Pakal, ruler of Palenque, emerges as a cacao tree. (Rubbing from Late Classic Maya stone sarcophagus lid, Temple of Inscriptions, Palenque, Mexico)

period creation myths than the sixteenth-century Popol Vuh leads us to believe. An Early Classic period image on the fragment of a carved pot excavated at the site of Teotihuacan in the 1930s reinforces this possibility (fig. 1.21). It shows a blowgunner, perhaps one of the Hero Twins (who were both hunters), taking aim at a quetzal bird in a cacao tree.[28]

Figure 1.17   An unidentified lord holding a cacao tree. (Late Classic jadeite plaque recovered from the Chichen Itza cenote)

Figure 1.18   The flower god, Ahaw Nik,
clutches a cacao tree as if it were a staff.
(Madrid Codex)

Figure 1.19   A mortuary scene of a maize god impersonator transforming into a cacao tree. (Early Classic Maya incised cylindrical vase)

Figure 1.20   The head of the maize god Hunahpú grows from the trunk of a cacao tree. A "humanoid" cacao pod (upper left corner) grows from another tree. (Late Classic Maya cylindrical vase)

Figure 1.21   A blowgunner, possibly one of the Hero Twins, hunting quetzal birds in a cacao tree. (Fragment of Early Classic tripod vase from Teotihuacan)

cacao for the gods

Deities often appear with the cacao tree, or its beans, pods, chocolate, and glyphic symbols, in some form of interaction. In Maya almanacs, such as the Dresden and Madrid codices (which chart solar and lunar eclipses and Venus cycles), deities use chocolate or cacao pods in their divination rituals.[29] Figure 1.22 shows the seductive moon goddess IxChel exchanging chocolate with Chac, a cave-dwelling, lecherous-looking rain god. Between them sits a large pot with two cacao glyphs on the front. The small gourd containers floating above their hands and on top of the pot most likely contain liquid chocolate. IxChel appears to be seducing Chac with a come-hither look, but more likely they are negotiating a deal. Earth's fertility and growing seasons may have been thought to depend on alliances between such gods, whose job it was to ensure that the rain would fall and the moon would continue its cycles. The collaboration between these two powerful personified forces, the moon and the rain, is facilitated here with chocolate as the central bargaining chip; as a negotiable commodity, it greased the wheels and made the world go round.

In the Dresden Codex, a series of creator gods acting as diviners handled cacao beans and cacao pods in prognostication rituals that foretold the positive or negative outcome of each day. Chac, with his legendary downturned nose, appears in at least two of these scenes. In figure 1.23, he holds a dish of cacao beans and is seated next to the god of sacrifice and war, who is also offering cacao pods. In a second scene (not shown), Chac offers a bowl of both cacao beans and pods and sits adjacent to the skeletal death god, who holds cacao pods.[30]

In figure 1.24, the Maya creator god, Itzamna, patron of all shamans, holds a cacao glyph encircled by dotted lines. In his magic, Itzamna was thought to bring forth sacred substances called *itz*, including a viscous sap, nectar, blood, sweat, semen, and tears.[31] The scene portrayed in the Dresden Codex may identify chocolate as one of these itz substances.

In another divination scene (not shown), the god K'awil is seated next to the maize god and holds a bowl of cacao beans in his hands. With upturned nose, burning torch on his forehead, and serpent foot, K'awil is most often identified with lightning, fire, and dynasty lineage.[32] But he is also closely associated with abundance, as his name in the Yucatec language, which translates as "sustenance" or "alms," indicates. He represents any precious substance such as sap, blood, or other fluids freely offered to the divine as a token of appeasement.[33] K'awil, in his association with abundance, is

*Figure 1.22   The rain god Chac and the
moon goddess IxChel exchange cacao.
(Madrid Codex)*

Figure 1.23 Chac with a cacao offering. (Dresden Codex)

Figure 1.24 Itzamna with an offering of cacao glyphs. (Dresden Codex)

*Figure 1.25   Maya gods shedding blood from
their ears onto cacao pods. (Madrid Codex)*

often depicted on painted capstones in the Puuc region of Yucatan with cacao beans
or pods (see chap. 3).

In addition, gods perform sacrificial acts involving cacao in the Madrid Codex.
In figure 1.25, four deities pierce their ears with obsidian blades, sprinkling the blood
onto cacao pods that lie on the ground. The gods in this image are important ones:
Itzamna (the outer left and right frames), the earth goddess Ixil Kab' (the left-center
frame) and the flower god Ahaw Nik (the right-center frame). But images of gods
with offerings of cacao were not limited solely to images in pictorial manuscripts or
on ceramics. A painted diving-god effigy vase (fig. 1.26), possibly from Postclassic
Tulum, juxtaposes cacao with corn motifs, in what may be another example of cacao-
corn dualism and synchrony. Diving gods are common figures found in Postclassic
Yucatan and the northern Maya lowlands; some researchers believe that they represent a Yucatec version of the maize god shown with stylized maize plants sprouting
from the top of the head.[34] This figure emerges from the open beak of a bird (or possibly from an eagle helmet); the bent, winglike legs straddle the vase in a descend-
ing position with the soles of the feet facing upward.[35] A cacao pod rests in the god's

Figure 1.26   A diving god with a cacao pod offering, accompanied by maize motifs. (Postclassic Maya painted vase from a region near Tulum, Mexico)

cupped hands in an attitude of supplication, while two maizelike plants adorn his head like a crown.

These pictorial legacies from Mesoamerica are dramatic indications that chocolate and the cacao tree had a special status in pre-Columbian religion and myth. Cacao was deified, while becoming an offering between the gods as well as between humans and gods. As a metaphorical World Tree, it provided a conduit between human and sacred realms and was integral to maintaining cycles of life, death, and rebirth at both earthly and supernatural levels. Cacao's deified role ensured its destiny as "food of the gods," casting it into a world of human ritual and ceremony for thousands of years to come.

chocolate and Ritual in Mesoamerica:
Fertility, Life Cycles, and the Soul's Journey

2

In the month of planting corn, we have to, as I told you, we have to drink some chocolate.

And that's very important. If you don't have chocolate drinks, I hear it is not good, but I don't

know how true it is, I didn't try it yet. But mostly before I plant corn I do my chocolate.

Caretaker of Blue Creek Cave, Belize, November 2001

Contemporary reliance on chocolate as a guarantee for a good corn harvest goes to the very core of a more ancient ritual system in which cacao offerings helped keep the sun on its course and the balance of nature intact. Whether within a cave, on ancient ballcourts, or in the Catholic church of contemporary Comalcalco during cacao harvest, these offerings appease gods and departed human souls alike.

Cacao and chocolate appear within a variety of ceremonial contexts, ranging from agrarian and calendrical events that follow critical celestial passages, to ones that impart sacredness to the most basic of human rites such as birth, death, and marriage (fig. 2.1). Some even involve

Figure 2.1   An altar with cups of chocolate and "first fruits" offered to the angels in Zacualpan, Guerrero, in 1994.

human sacrifice and blood. These rites revolve around human dialogue with supernatural entities whose regenerative powers can bring—if the gods are so inclined—seasonal and human renewal. Offerings of sacred cacao, what the Chorti Maya call their *awas peq*, have kept the dialogue flowing and the favorable odds on the side of humanity.[1]

cacao offerings in caves and sinkholes

Today in the Maya Mountains of southern Belize, villagers gather in the dark recesses of Blue Creek Cave and other nearby caves to pay respect to the cave deities prior to planting corn. It is essential that chocolate and other food items be left on an altar inside the caverns so that the supernaturals can smell their aromas. After three days, the chocolate and food are removed and buried near the cemetery. The cave's caretaker, Sulvano Sho, warns that when farmers ignore these ancient customs, bad things can happen to both crops and people.

For well over five thousand years, Mesoamerican caves have been religious and ceremonial focal points.[2] These geological formations were considered sources of life, fertility, abundance, and power, for not only did underground rivers originate in them, but in dry areas (such as the Yucatan), caves and large sinkholes, called cenotes, were often the only vital source of fresh water.[3] It is not surprising, then, that cave symbolism appears with great frequency in pre-Columbian art, architecture, and writing. The earliest known depictions are on Olmec monuments where deities and leaders (i.e., the religious and secular elite) emerge from cave entrances, doorways to the Underworld. The cave imagery on the Classic period Maya vase in figure 4.7 continues this symbolism: on the far left, Itzamna is seated within a cave opening in front of a vessel, which perhaps contains chocolate.

As a sacred "meeting ground between humans and the divine," caves served as portals to an Underworld realm to which souls traveled after death and where frightful earth and rain gods resided.[4] From these quarters, the gods orchestrated lightning, wind, and rain—no small matter, given human reliance on seasonal cycles and successful harvests. To reach these deities, acts of appeasement were always necessary. Archaeologists have found offertory cacao or ceramic representations of cacao in caves. In one cave located in the Maya Mountains of southern Belize, Keith Prufer and his team found a modeled cacao pod, probably broken off of a larger incense burner.[5]

Another example was painted on a capstone found in the ruins of the Temple of the Owls at Chichen Itza in Yucatan (fig. 2.2).[6] On it, K'awil, Maya god of abundance, emerges from the open jaws of an Underworld serpent into a U-shaped cenote enclosure. He holds an offertory platter of chocolate balls and several flasklike gourds with stoppers, probably filled with liquid chocolate. Celestial bands frame K'awil on either side, indicating that he has entered the celestial realm with his offerings. Above him, a band of undeciphered text may possibly end in a glyph for cacao. Hanging from the

Figure 2.2   K'awil in a cenote with suspended cacao pods. He emerges from the Underworld with offerings of chocolate-filled gourds. (Late Classic Maya painted capstone from the Temple of the Owls, Chichen Itza)

walls and ceilings of this enclosure are cacao pods, ancient verification that cenotes are an ideal microclimate for cacao growth.[7]

The Jaguar: Protector of cacao

Both feared and revered, the jaguar commanded a powerful presence within Mesoamerican mythology and became a spirit companion for shamans. His unique status made him a prized sacrificial offering. As a creature of the night with starlike spots, he was also a mythological Underworld god, representing the nighttime sun, moving from west to east and retreating into caves to sleep at daybreak.[8] Cave entries are often portrayed as the open jaw of some wild beast with zoomorphic features such as those of a serpent or jaguar, the open mouth alluding to the penetration of the earth into a sacred realm (fig. 2.3).

The jaguar's nocturnal routine of roaming in and out of the cacao trees within rainforests may have aligned it symbolically with cacao, perhaps as a guardian. This feline's association with cacao was further reinforced by its habit of resting in the tree's limbs, possibly waiting to prey on the pesky monkeys that shamelessly yank the cacao pods from the tree to get at the tasty pulp inside. In several Maya languages, the

Figure 2.3   A cave mouth resembling the open jaws of a jaguar or other wild beast. (Chanona Cave, Belize)

Chapter Two

name for a particular kind of cacao (*pataxte*, or *Theobroma bicolor*) is *balam-té*, or "jaguar tree."[9] Even today, *balam* or *balam-té* continues to be the name for pataxte in the Alta Verapaz region of Guatemala.

In this highland region, a spectacular incensario lid of a modeled jaguar was discovered. The jaguar is perched on what appears to be a spiked ceiba tree trunk; he wears a collar adorned with two cacao pods, which may indicate that he serves as a sacrifice (fig. 2.4). Also, at El Baúl, Guatemala, in the once-cacao-rich Cotzumalhuapa archaeological area near the Pacific coast, a jaguar with nine attached cacao pods is carved in low relief on one side of Monument 4 (fig. 2.5). This image seems to be associated with the concept of a jaguar tree, with pods growing from the "body" of the tree.[10] Yet the entire scene is one of sacrifice and violence, reflecting the jaguar's sacrificial value. The dying jaguar has a long forked tongue, indicative of death, and a "cruller" (the twisted icon affixed to the top of his eyes), the mark of a supernatural being. He wears what may be a sacrificial scarf around his neck.

Figure 2.4   A jaguar, wearing a collar of suspended cacao pods, perched atop a ceiba tree trunk. (Maya open bowl censer from highland Guatemala)

Figure 2.5   a (above): A sacrificial jaguar (lower left) with cacao pods attached to its body. b (below): A line drawing of the jaguar image on the monument. (Late Classic Maya, stone Monument 4, El Baúl, Cotzumalhuapa area, Esquintla, Guatemala)

Cacao: The Mesoamerican Ballgame, Sacrifice, and Blood

Imagery of cacao pods and ballgame scenes appear together on monuments at various sites throughout the ancient cacao-growing areas along the Pacific piedmonts of Chiapas and Guatemala, a region with one of the highest concentrations of known ballcourts.[11] The earliest dated court (1400–1250 BC), at Paso de la Amada, Chiapas, even predates Olmec influence.[12] Mesoamerican ballgame symbolism is complex and multidimensional. On one level, it was entertainment, a venue for intense wagering or a way to settle disputes between rival powers over land or political issues.[13] On a cosmic level, the sport's ritual overtones became paramount, ending in decapitation and human sacrifice.[14] Even its architecture, when viewed as a cross section, resembles the stepped, open jaws of a serpent, a metaphorical entrance into the Underworld.

On Monument 21 (fig. 2.6) at Bilbao, also in the Cotzumalhuapa area near El Baúl, a narrative scene depicts a central ballplayer, a goateed sorcerer on the left with a puppet, and a seated priestlike human figure on the right. Winding in and out of the scene are flowering vines to which anthropomorphic cacao pods and other stylized motifs are attached. The central ballplayer figure holds a sacrificial knife in one hand and a personified cacao pod in the other, while the seated figure holds a personified pod in each hand.[15]

Monument 3, one of eight so-called Ball-Player Stelae from Bilbao, is a scene of sacrifice and death in which a central ballplayer offers a personified cacao pod to a diving deity, perhaps a sun god (fig. 2.7). A small skeletal body to his right points upward, either to a disembodied head on a trophy rack or to the diving god. The upraised pod may symbolize a sacrificial heart or perhaps a decapitated head as a sacrificial offering. Sacrifice of ballplayers was a reality of the ballgame. Even the Quiché Maya term for the rubber ball, *quic*, is the same word for blood, a term used in the Popol Vuh.[16]

Cacao and ballgame iconography also appear together on Mexico's Gulf Coast in northern Veracruz, at El Tajin, a site with at least eighteen ballcourts. On Panel 1 at the Pyramid of the Niches, a ballplayer ascends a stepped platform while holding a harvesting stick, a familiar forked implement still used today for knocking cacao pods from tree limbs (fig. 2.8). Opposite him, a seated figure petting a feline or monkey has a headdress supporting a skeletal image with an open chest cavity, suggesting heart extraction. Perhaps like several of the Bilbao monuments discussed above, the cacao tree in this panel may represent rejuvenation, an outcome of ballgame sacrifice.

Sixteenth-century chroniclers of Aztec and Maya life were quick to recognize the symbolic connections between the cacao pod and chocolate, and the heart and blood.

The cacao pod may have replaced the human heart as an offering because both the heart and the heart-shaped cacao pod served as repositories for precious liquids—blood and chocolate.[17] The Spanish chronicler Gonzalo Fernandez de Oviedo y Valdés, observing that Nicaraguans added *achiote* to their chocolate to color it red, stated that the people there had a "taste for human blood."[18] Icons of bleeding cacao, in fact, appear in Mixtec codices and other manuscripts as part of toponyms, or place-names, of villages (fig. 2.9). Exactly why bleeding cacao represented certain villages is unclear, but perhaps these places were locations of sacrificial activity.

Figure 2.6   A ballplayer (the large central figure) holding a "personified" cacao pod while surrounded by anthropomorphic cacao pods on vines. (Late Classic Maya, stone Monument 21, Bilbao, Cotzumalhuapa area, Esquintla, Guatemala)

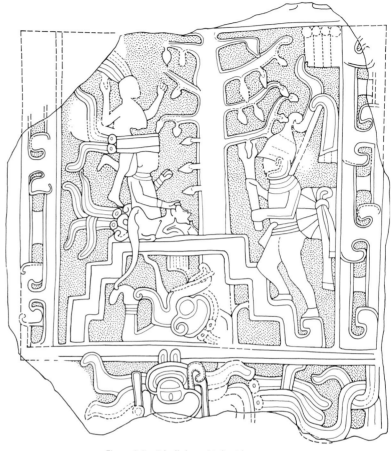

Figure 2.8   A ballplayer (right side, ascending the steps) carrying a cacao harvesting stick. (Late Classic Maya carved stone, Panel 1, Pyramid of the Niches, El Tajin, Veracruz)

Figure 2.7   A Maya ballplayer offering a cacao pod to a diving god. (Late Classic Maya stone stela, Monument 3, from Bilbao, Cotzumalhuapa area, Esquintla, Guatemala)

Figure 2.9   A glyph of the Mixtec place-name of Teozacoalco, containing the image of bleeding cacao, detail from a map in the sixteenth-century "Relación Geografica de Teozacoalco" (JGI XXV-3).

cacao and calendrical cycles: New Fire Rituals and Renewal

Obsession with time and calendrical events fueled rituals during which cacao offerings helped to ensure the continuation of cosmic and agricultural cycles. One, called the New Fire ceremony, occurred on the five nameless days of Wayeb, or Uayeb, which followed the 360-day year of the Mesoamerican calendar. Considered dangerous, these unnamed days were filled with uncertainty as to whether the sun would rise for the following year.[19]

Often New Fire ceremonies and cacao pods were graphically paired. In the Mixtec Codex Vindobonensis, "bleeding" cacao pods are offered with three other items during a mythological creation represented by repetitive building cycles (fig. 2.10), each sanctified with New Fire rituals. Palaces, temples, sweat baths, and ballcourts were created; when this long creation sequence ended, the Mixteca world was finally ready for human occupation.[20] New Fire ceremonies also accompanied calendrical celebrations at the end of each *k'atun*, or twenty-year cycle, and sometimes images of cacao trees and fire glyphs appear together to reflect this. On a series of Teotihuacan-influenced cylinder tripod vases found in tombs at Kaminaljuyu, Guatemala, bands of comb and bar signs resembling the Maya glyph for fire (or a bundle of wood), *k'ak*, appear with stylized cacao trees. Figure 1.8 shows the comb and bar signs along the lower band of the vase.[21]

Maya New Year rituals performed during the five dangerous days of Wayeb revolve around the deification of a strange multipersona entity called Mam ("grandfather," "ancient one") or MaXimón. The historian Diego Lopez de Cogolludo wrote in 1688 that the Yucatec Maya had a wooden figure they called Mam, which they dressed and sat on a stool, offering it food and drink during the Wayeb, only to discard it with irreverence after the fifth day.[22] What they fed Mam is not clear, but if twentieth-century observations give us any clue, Mam's food of choice would have been chocolate.

In Santiago Atitlan, Guatemala, Mam resembles the "Old Merchant Lord" with his large Stetson hat and long cigar (fig. 2.11), taking on the provocative and rowdy nature of God L, the Maya merchant god from the Classic period, patron god of cacao (fig. 2.12). Mam's body is carved from the sacred *tz'ajtel*, or coral tree (*Erythrina corallodendron*), the "talking tree" and guardian of cacao trees in this area. Bundled together with rope, Mam binds the old year to the new during the five dangerous days of Wayeb that coincide with Holy Week, Semana Santa, preceding Easter.

Cacao and other fruits are gathered for Mam during a pilgrimage of young male initiates to the coast, replicating a journey probably as ancient as the merchant god

Figure 2.10 Bleeding cacao pods offered in the temple on the far left (in the middle band) during the New Fire ritual, signifying creation of the Mixtec world. (Codex Vindobonensis)

Figure 2.11 MaXimón, or Mam, "waiting" for cacao and other "first fruits" during Semana Santa in Santiago Atitlan, Guatemala.

himself. Traveling by foot to the place of the ancient cacao groves on the Wednesday before Semana Santa, they return with their *kakaxtle*, framed packs filled with cacao fruits (both *Theobroma cacao* and *Theobroma bicolor*) and other fruits. "Fed" to Mam in the middle of Holy Week, these fruits will sustain him on his long journey through the Underworld after his impending sacrifice. Immediately "hung" and dismantled, Mam is then "rejuvenated" when Jesus dies on Friday, as a newly bound Mam for the New Year.[23]

The syncretic celebration of the Maya New Year within the guise of Semana Santa is equally alive and well in many other parts of Guatemala today. And it is little wonder, for both these religious events originated from an agrarian calendar governed by

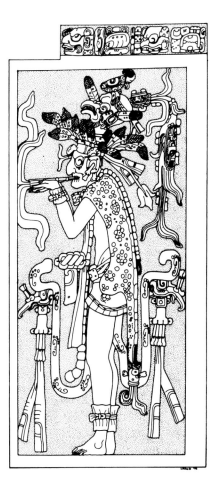

Figure 2.12   God L, the merchant god,
with his identifying cigar, muan bird
headdress, and jaguar-pelt cloak.
(Temple of the Cross, Palenque)

the spring equinox.[24] In the area surrounding Santiago Atitlan, the forty-day fasting period before Easter falls at the end of the dry season, when cacao growing along the Pacific slope is harvested and maize is planted. Mam is lord of the dry season, and thus cacao; Jesus, of the wet season, and thus corn. This complementary relationship between the cacao- and corn-growing cycles is reflected time and time again, as in figure 2.13, which shows cacao pods growing from the maize god, who emerges from "Split Place."

Termination and renewal ceremonies using chocolate as propitiation to the gods acquire an altogether different form in the Lacandon Chol Maya region of Chiapas, Mexico, where cacao trees of a rare vinelike species grow in the forest.[25] Vested in

Figure 2.13   A maize god with cacao pods attached to his body, emerging from the "split place" mountain. (Late Classic Maya ceramic whistle)

Figure 2.14   A painted god pot, sacred effigy of hacekyum *("our true lord"). (Maya-Lacandon, Chiapas, Mexico)*

pre-Columbian rituals, the Lacandon have continued to use clay effigy incense burners, or "god pots," as a medium by which to transmit their offerings and gifts. At least as late as the 1980s, old god pots from the previous year were ceremonially "killed" and abandoned before their replacements were imbued with powers of transmission.[26] Both old and new god pots were "fed" with ritual offerings of *pom* incense, meat-filled tortillas, drinks of corn pozole and *balche* (made from fermented bark of the balche tree), and always chocolate.

During the Classic period, god pots were called *ol*, or "center," "heart of," indicating their role as portals to the Otherworld.[27] Imbued with grotesque, abstract facial features representing specific gods, the pots were painted with decorative elements using the blood-red dye of the *achiote,* ensouling them with life force (fig. 2.14).[28] Five cacao beans placed in the bowl of each new god pot represented his heart, lungs, liver, stomach, and diaphragm.[29]

The method of presenting chocolate to these god pots has varied throughout the centuries, as has the ceremony. A seventeenth-century manuscript created for the president of the Spanish *audiencia* (a judicial district that controlled Guatemala,

Chiapas, and portions of Central America) in Guatemala recounts that during "the feast of the cigarettes," the priests "rubbed well the snout of the idols with the fat of the animals, and they give them (the idols) ground cacao to drink."[30] The early-twentieth-century archaeologist Alfred E. Tozzer observed that old and new god pots were given frothed chocolate, mixed either with pozole or the balche drinks as final offerings.[31] In a late-twentieth-century account, the god pots were given a "sneak preview" of the cacao beans prior to receiving their frothy chocolate. The women prepared the mixture with a special grass (*sugir*) that acts as a foaming agent and, to ensure frothing success, sang a special frothing song.[32]

cacao and Agricultural rituals

Agrarian rituals for cacao and other foods reflect an ancient earth clock, rooted in the movement of the sky and the path of the sun. In many instances, chocolate offerings ensure a bountiful maize crop. In portions of eastern Guatemala, the Chorti Maya still conduct rain ceremonies in late April before planting maize; in these ceremonies, *chilate*, a drink composed of three sacred ingredients (maize, cacao, and virgin water, that is, water taken from caves or hollows), is the primary offering. In one such ceremony, witnessed in the mid-twentieth century, four directional corners were staked out on the ground around a central hole representing the navel of the earth. Five bowls of chilate and the blood of a sacrificed turkey were offered to the earth gods through the hole, "feeding" the earth to fertilize it.[33]

Rituals and festivals also prevailed before and after cacao harvests. Some sixteenth-century accounts reveal diverse forms of sacrifice and self-sacrifice to guarantee a bountiful cacao crop. In the ancient town of Xeoj (San Bartolomé), for example, people offered blood from their ears and arms to the earth deities to ensure good weather at the onset of the blooming of the cacao flowers, much like the deities in the Madrid Codex in figure 1.25.[34]

In cacao-growing regions near the Pacific coast, Oviedo y Valdés described the only documented account of a unique celebration at the end of a cacao harvest. In honor of their cacao god, Cacaguate, the Pipil-Nicarao of Nicaragua performed a *volador* ceremony. After exuberant dancing, human flyers tethered to a tall pole "flew" around a brightly painted idol of Cacaguate secured to the platform at the top.[35]

In the dry region of the Yucatan, where the only hospitable environment for cacao growth was that of cenotes, Diego de Landa in the sixteenth century observed during the month of Muan such a harvest festival hosted by cacao plantation owners honor-

Figure 2.15   A contemporary garment made from cacao beans and leaves. (Comalcalco, Mexico, 2000)

ing the patron deities of cacao: Ek Chuah, Chac, and Hobnil.[36] "To do this they went to the property of one of them, where they sacrificed a dog, spotted with the colors of the cacao, burned incense to their idols, and offered up iguanas of the blue sort with certain blue feathers, and other game, then they gave to each one of the officers a branch of the cacao fruit. After the sacrifice and prayers they ate the gifts and drank."[37]

Today, no festival in Mexico better reflects the continuation of these ancient harvest rituals than the Fiesta de San Isidro Enrama in contemporary Comalcalco, Tabasco. As May heralds the end of the dry season and the time of cacao harvest, the town erupts into a celebratory frenzy honoring the Catholic patron of agriculture, San Isidro Labrador. Costumes of cacao beans and tree leaves are specifically created for this event (fig. 2.15). Thousands of multicolored cacao pods from the outlying cacao plantations are lashed to long branches called *enramas*, which are then tied to trucks, horse carts, and even bicycles decorated with flowers and fruit. These vehicles join thousands of people with their cacao-laden enramas parading through the streets as the cacao pods are offered to the church and to San Isidro as tithe payment (fig. 2.16). As the whole community is pulled together in an elaborate display of gratitude and celebration, the priest blesses the offerings with holy water on the church steps before the enramas are stacked near the pews inside the church. Near the altar, necklaces of strung cacao beans cover the statue of San Isidro as each participant moves close to touch, or kiss, the feet of their agricultural patron (fig. 2.17). Like Ek Chuah, the pre-Columbian patron god of cacao, San Isidro is revered as a patron of cacao. Outside, a local *pozol* drink of ground cacao, corn, water, and spices is served to the parishioners almost as a sacramental communion. Early the next morning, after a night of revelry and dancing, church members and priests proceed to a nearby processing plant to extract the cacao beans from truckloads of cacao pods. After fermentation and drying, these cacao beans are later sold at the market, with proceeds benefiting the church. Down the road, at the church altar in the town of Cupilco, a statue of the Virgin Mary has been laden with necklaces of cacao beans similar to San Isidro's adornment; it recalls the ancient image of Cacao Woman (fig. 2.18).

Figure 2.16 (opposite, and following page)
Four views of the Fiesta de San Isidro
Enrama in Comalcalco, Mexico, in 2000.

Figure 2.16 (continued)   Views of the Fiesta de San Isidro Enrama in Comalcalco, Mexico, in 2000.

Figure 2.17 A statue of San Isidro Labrador adorned with strands of cacao beans in Comalcalco.

Figure 2.18 A statue of the Virgin in the church of Cupilco, adorned with strands of cacao beans. (Cupilco, Tabasco, Mexico)

The Taboo Tree: social ceremonies and rites of passage

In the 1930s, anthropologist Ruth Bunzel uncovered a curious Quiché Maya legend wherein the cacao tree was considered a taboo tree. The story combines Maya and Christian mythology and sheds some light on why cacao and chocolate must be reserved as a sacred food for important ceremonies. The tale suggests that Christ, pursued by his enemies, took refuge under a cacao tree, which immediately covered him with a blanket of white cacao blossoms, hiding him from his tormentors. Christ, thankful for his sanctuary, blessed the cacao tree. He decreed that the tree's wood would never be used for firewood—a kind of environmental sanction—and that cacao and chocolate would appear at the tables of all ceremonies. This myth reflects how the ritual food of a conquered culture found its way into the heart of Christianity and sanctified events.

Cacao seeds and chocolate have been offered in marriage negotiations and ceremonies throughout Mesoamerican history. In a palace scene painted on a Classic period Maya vase from Dos Pilas, Guatemala, marriage negotiations appear to be in progress. Two negotiators offer bouquets of earflowers (*Cymbopetalum penduliflorum*), an ingredient for wedding chocolate, to a seated lord. A vessel of chocolate sits in front of the seated lord (fig. 2.19). Another image, from the Codex Nuttall, depicts an AD 1051 Mixtec marriage in which Lord Eight Deer receives a frothy jar of chocolate from his bride, Lady Thirteen Serpent (fig. 2.20). The drink symbolizes the Mixtec phrase for royal marriage: "a royal vessel was placed before the nobleman."[38]

Opposite:

Figure 2.19 (above)   A marriage negotiation in a palace scene, with a presentation of earflowers. (Late Classic Maya cylindrical vase)

Figure 2.20 (below)   The Mixtec marriage of Lord Eight Deer and Lady Thirteen Serpent, who exchange a cup of chocolate. (Codex Nuttall)

In the sixteenth century, cacao seeds were commonly used as legal currency for a marriage dowry, or bride price.[39] But in today's communities, where exchanges of cacao and chocolate still symbolically validate marriage negotiations and ceremonies, the monetary value of such gifts is negligible. In Chichicastenango during the 1930s, twenty-five to thirty cacao seeds were the first gift brought to the parents of the bride by the negotiator. Acceptance of this gift signaled the parents' approval of the marriage proposal.[40] Among the Q'eqchi Maya during the 1980s, the same held true; the fiancée agrees to the marriage proposal if she accepts the chocolate. During the marriage ceremony that ensues, the groom gives the bride thirteen seeds of cacao, signifying the thirteen great hills in Q'eqchi mythology.[41]

Today's Mopan Maya in the Toledo District of southern Belize continue this tradition. Cacao seeds given by the groom's family to the bride's are ground into chocolate and made into a drink by the bride's mother or other females of the household, then are served to the family of the groom as they come to negotiate. Here, too, acceptance of the gift indicates the willingness of the bride's family to agree to the marriage offer. Sometimes several visits are necessary, and each negotiation visit requires a ritual gift of cacao. Later, at the wedding, drinks of chocolate are an essential component of the marriage feast.

Ceremonial presentations of cacao can begin much earlier in life, at birth and baptism rites. Among the sixteenth-century Pipil-Nicarao, cacao and fowls were offered twelve days after birth when the baby was named. Afterwards, while the mother bathed the baby in a river, she offered cacao and copal to the river to divert evil from her child.[42] In various communities of twentieth-century Guatemala, cacao has been served at a little feast twenty days following birth, as well as being presented to the designated godparents before and after birth and immediately after baptism. In Yucatan, chocolate was ceremonially drunk when a man consented to be a godfather.[43] A similar Oaxacan custom involves the offering of many kilograms of chocolate by the godparents to the parents of their godchild.[44]

Fray Diego de Landa in the sixteenth century witnessed a Maya baptism at which cacao was used as in the scene from the Madrid Codex shown in figure 2.21.[45] The Maya children were draped in white cloths decorated with feathers and cacao seeds. A priest and four of the fathers representing Chacs ritually purified the house where the baptism was to occur. Then the priest, wearing a jacket and headdress of colored feathers and holding a brush of "hyssop," an aromatic plant, and rattlesnake-like tails, covered each child's head with a white cloth. He wet a bone with water and "anointed

them on their foreheads and the features of their faces, as well as the spaces between the fingers and toes." The anointing water was unlike any holy water known to Catholic priests; it was "made from certain flowers and of cacao pounded and dissolved in virgin water," taken "from the hollows of the trees or of the rocks in the forests."[46]

Today in Coban, Guatemala, where chocolate drinks continue to be called *kakaw*, guests on special occasions are ceremoniously greeted with the sound of firecrackers and are led to the house on a pathway of pine needles and roses. The host welcomes them with a blessing over coarsely ground chocolate drinks served in small, brightly painted calabash cups (*joom*) that are reserved for chocolate (see fig. 4.31).

In ceremonies with religious overtones, only young children are "pure" enough to serve the kakaw drink (fig. 2.22). Nana Winters, a spiritual leader of Coban, performed one such ceremony, observed by one of the authors in the fall of 2004. After an elaborate process of roasting and grinding the cacao beans and mixing the resulting chocolate paste with water, cinnamon, anise, and sugar, participants were served their small cup of cacao drink by a young boy and girl. Drawing a circular quincunx

Figure 2.21   A Maya ritual resembling baptism. (Madrid Codex)

Figure 2.22   A child serving chocolate in highland Guatemala.

cosmogram (four corners with a center point) on the ground with sugar, Señora Winters placed four different colored candles at each of the cardinal directions and in the center. Copal incense and wildflowers from the mountains and the countryside were also placed within the circle. Following appeals for personal strength, participants threw sesame seeds, sugar, and rum into the circle, enflaming the *ocote*-lit fire at its center. These gifts symbolically gave the earth something in return, in hopes that the appeals would be granted. A slow, small-stepped dance repeated three times around the fire-lit quincunx ended the ceremony that was initiated by chocolate (fig. 2.23).

Figure 2.23   Cacao ceremony performed by Nana Winters with a quincunx cosmogram delineating the four cardinal directions and center axis mundi. (Coban, Guatemala)

chocolate and cacao accompany the soul's journey

It was in matters of death, however, that cacao and chocolate took on cosmic dimensions. Horrific accounts from sixteenth-century European explorers give us a glimpse into this powerful aspect of chocolate. One shocked observer, for example, recanted an Aztec ceremony in which "last rite" cacao concoctions, often dyed blood-red, were administered to the sacrificial victims before their hearts were extracted.[47] Chocolate thus was not only coveted by gods and rulers but also served the human soul after death in the trials and tribulations of a supernatural Underworld.

The notion that chocolate energized and eased the soul's journey is an ancient concept, dating to 600–400 BC, if not older. The earliest indisputable proof that cacao/chocolate was provided for the deceased at the time of burial comes from the Maya site of Colha, Belize, where spouted ceramic vessels once containing chocolate accompanied burials (see fig. 4.9).[48]

From Río Azul, another Maya site in Guatemala, a team from the University of Texas at San Antonio unearthed a fifth-century burial tomb in 1986. The undisturbed tomb had painted walls and contained the skeletal remains of a nobleman accompanied by fourteen ceramic vessels that had originally held food. One small vessel stood out as particularly exquisite; it was a polychrome and stuccoed pot with a rare, "child-proof," interlocking lid (fig. 2.24). After epigrapher David Stuart had deciphered the glyph for cacao on the pot's painted surface, archaeologist Grant Hall scraped residue samples from the pot's interior and sent them to the Hershey Chocolate Company's lab for chemical analysis.[49] (Though this is now a common procedure, Hall was the first to send archaeological samples to Hershey's.) The results were positive—the small vessel and two other cylindrical vases, some with liquid lines still apparent, had indeed held chocolate.[50]

Under normal circumstances (i.e., not a sealed tomb), it is extremely rare to find cacao remains in archaeological contexts because they decompose. But a discovery by Keith Prufer at Batsub Cave in southern Belize is an exciting exception. About AD 250, a shaman was interred in a remote area of the cave; he wore an elaborate jade and shell necklace and was surrounded by beautiful ceramics. As Prufer later recounted to the authors, "His head was cut off and placed in his lap. A bowl of cacao beans was placed upside down in his lap along with the head [fig. 2.25]. And then where his head was, they put another bowl and they put a jade bead on it."[51]

Why was a shaman buried with a bowl of cacao beans in his lap? Were they part of his shamanistic tool kit, or were they needed for his afterlife journey? Although we may never know for sure, archaeological findings of cacao and chocolate offerings with the dead are supported by similar events recorded in pre-Columbian codices. One illustration of a pre-Hispanic funeral scene appears in the Codex Nuttall (fig. 2.26). It portrays the death and funeral procession of Twelve Movement, Lord Eight Deer's older half brother. An individual (bottom center) is offering a vessel brimming with foaming cacao at the funeral.[52]

Throughout Mexico today, vestiges of pre-Columbian rites of death and cacao offerings survive in many forms. In Pisa Flores, Veracruz, during the week prior to

Figure 2.24 A chocolate
vessel. (Early Classic Maya
painted and stuccoed
pot with lock-top lid
from Tomb 19 at Rio Azul,
Guatemala)

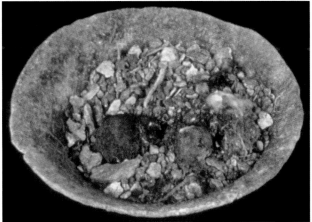

Figure 2.25 A bowl containing cacao
beans, found with an Early Classic shaman
burial in Batsub Cave, Belize.

Figure 2.26   A chocolate offering (bottom center) at the funeral scene of Twelve Movement. The murder of Twelve Movement in pictured in the lower right. His body is bundled in the upper right. (Codex Nuttall)

Lent, turkey mole made with chocolate, peanuts, and various chilies is integral to a curious version of the Día de los Muertos, or Day of the Dead, rituals. It honors the newly departed souls of those who are believed to have gone to hell and are expected to become devils, usually those who have died under nefarious circumstances—criminals, murderers, and, with certainty, policemen. About fourteen to twenty "devils" travel to the homes of the recently deceased to welcome them into "devilhood." Not wanting devils inside, the relatives of the deceased have set up Day of the Dead–type altars outside their houses, with mole, beer, and personal things, including clothes and shoes belonging to the deceased (fig. 2.27). After "dancing the clothing," the visiting devils along with the souls of those departed are fed the mole and beer. They eat while squatting low or sitting on the ground to be closer to hell. Afterwards, an X is drawn on the ground with the chocolate mole sauce (fig. 2.28) in honor of the offering, and the devils then run to the next house at breakneck speed to welcome the next initiate.[53]

Figure 2.27   An altar with chocolate mole *offerings to deceased devil souls, in Pisa Flores, Mexico, in 1997.*

Figure 2.28   An X of mole on the ground in Pisa Flores in 1997.

Figure 2.29   A children's altar with cups of chocolate for the Day of the Dead in Huautla, Hildalgo, in 1991.

Figure 2.30 A Day of the Dead altar with cups of chocolate in San Pedro Tziltzacuapan, Hildalgo, in 1996.

The most renowned example of linking chocolate to celebrations of the dead, however, is the Day of the Dead. Coinciding with the Christian observance of All Saints' Day and All Souls' Day (November 1–2) of each year, family members honor their deceased ancestors. The souls of the deceased are thought to return for a few hours to spend time with the living and to indulge in earthly pleasures once enjoyed in life.

Oaxaca is renowned for this special occasion. Here, chocolate is everywhere during the preparations for the observance: at the cemetery, where family members drink chocolate, and at family altars in each household. Along with chocolate, other favorite food and drink such as *pan de muerte*, tamales, and tequila are placed on the altar for the returning ancestors to smell and enjoy, amidst memorabilia and photographs (fig. 2.29 and 2.30). After the departed souls have had "their fill," family members gather around the family table to enjoy and feast on the food and chocolate.

Dia de los Muertos may have origins in Aztec feasts for the dead, the "Little Feast" for children and the "Great Feast" for adults. These feasts were incorporated into the Christian All Saints' Day during the sixteenth century, with food, including chocolate, being offered.[54] Today, none of these ancient roots may be remembered, but chocolate, at least in Oaxaca, still seems to be a requirement. One Day of the Dead celebrant explained, "In this festival, chocolate is the main drink, for the living and the dead. Right now, I'm alive and I like chocolate. When I die, maybe the living will put out chocolate for me, because I liked it."

power, wealth, and greed:
The seduction of cacao

The cacao was in some bins like great cubes, made of wicker, so huge that six men could not span them, coated with clay inside and out, all placed in order, which was something to see. They serve as granaries . . . sometimes . . . closed on top and opened on one side . . . underneath a flat roof. Alonso de Ojeda, on seeing that daylight was on its way, before time ran out, cut the bands of those bins with a broadsword; then those looking for cacao stuffed their skirts and mantles; they emptied three bins, in [each of] which were 600 loads, each load having 24,000 beans.   Francisco Cervantes de Salazar, 1554

If the numbers recorded by Cervantes de Salazar are correct, Spanish soldiers and their native servants, under orders from the avaricious Pedro de Alvarado, looted 43,200,000 cacao beans while raiding Moctezuma's grand stockpile of riches at Tenochtitlan—an impressive amount but less than one-twentieth of the cacao in the Aztec ruler's possession![1] This dramatic account casts a harsh light on the greed generated by cacao and the prosperity and power it could provide, an allure that existed within Mesoamerica long before European contact.

wealth in the supernatural Realm

Chocolate may have fueled afterlife journeys, but what is more important is that it has greased the wheels of Mesoamerica's economy over several millennia. Classic period Maya art had long reinforced the intrinsic value of cacao by illustrating it in the company of influential deities who facilitated prosperity and fertility. K'awil and the Underworld God L, the wealthy merchant god of the Classic period, are primary subjects cast in this iconography.

Three painted and carved capstones recovered from Maya archaeological sites in the Campeche and Yucatan regions of Mexico juxtapose K'awil with cacao: a painted capstone from Chichen Itza (see fig. 2.2); the Dzibilnocac capstone from Campeche; and a painted capstone of unknown providence (fig. 3.1) having traits characteristic of Campeche style.[2] Often associated with prognostication rites or building dedications,

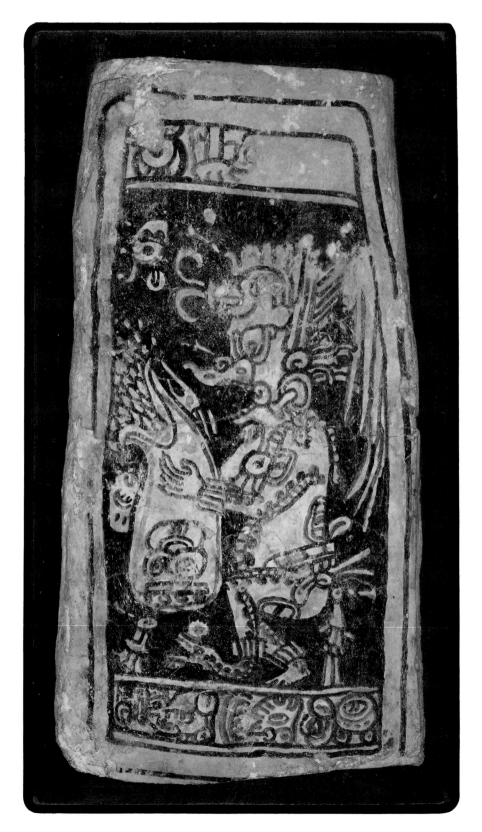

Figure 3.1   K'awil with a bag of cacao beans. A cacao glyph is in the middle of the band below. (Late Classic Maya painted capstone, Campeche region)

these painted capstones spanned the gap at the top between the two sides of a corbelled vault—a distinctive feature of Maya architecture—thus "closing" the dedicatory room below and representing, at least within a Maya ideological perspective, the portal through which the deity on the capstone could move from one world to the next.[3] Scenes of food offerings such as cacao by deities who represent fertility and wealth imbue these capstones with qualities of prosperity and reciprocity.

On the capstone in figure 3.1, the serpent-footed deity K'awil, while running or dancing, grasps a large sack overflowing with cacao beans as if to signify an overflow of abundance and wealth. The cacao glyph appears in the band at the bottom. Glyphs on the sack describe this "first" *carga* (or load) as abundant. If translated literally, these glyphs give us an exact count of beans: nine eight thousands, or 72,000 beans.[4]

Cacao as a symbolic marker of status and wealth appears on a Classic period vessel known as the Princeton Vase (fig. 3.2). In this supernatural palace scene, God L wears his identifying cape and large-brimmed hat topped by the *muan* bird. His wealth and opulent lifestyle are reinforced by the elaborate preparation of a chocolate beverage by a woman standing behind him, raising the foam as she pours the liquid chocolate from vase to vase.

Figure 3.2   A palace scene with God L (the large figure seated on the dais, right of center). A woman pouring chocolate (see detail in fig. 4.3) is behind him. An execution scene is pictured on the far left. (Late Classic Maya cylindrical vase)

An execution scene beyond God L may be a foreshadowing of impending doom: he owns cacao and has become very wealthy because of it, fostering jealousy within the supernatural realm. Scenes on other vases continue sagas of his eventual demise as various deities, envious of his wealth, strip this master and patron of cacao of all his riches and possessions in dramas of supernatural greed of Shakespearian proportions.[5]

Agricultural centers of cacao: Geographic and Environmental Realities

In the real world, the ownership of cacao production and control of its distribution created spheres of power and great wealth over the course of several thousand years. A difficult tree to grow, cacao requires humid tropical ecosystems within a narrow band twenty degrees north and south of the equator.[6] Within these latitude zones, cacao could be grown on both coasts of Mesoamerica (fig. 3.3). Three major pre-Columbian cacao-growing districts remained commercially viable in the sixteenth century, according to Spanish chroniclers: the Pacific coastal plain region of Chiapas and Guatemala, which included the Soconusco (Xoconusco) and Suchitepequez areas; the gulf coast region of Tabasco; and the Caribbean region of northwestern Honduras.

Secondary and scattered cacao-growing regions also existed along the gulf coast in Veracruz (extending into northern Oaxaca), along the Caribbean in northern Belize, and along the Pacific in El Salvador, Costa Rica, the Cihuatlan province in Guerrero, Colima, and Narayit.[7] Much of the cacao grown was for local consumption, such as in Colima, and thus was more widely accessible to commoners. In nonproducing areas of Mesoamerica that had to import cacao, the laws of supply and demand made it a luxury item available only to the elites.

Ancient farmers were ingenious in regions where dry seasons lasted longer than four months. For example, the Pipil-Nicarao peoples of Nahua origin (who migrated into the Central America regions of El Salvador, Honduras, Guatemala, and Nicaragua from AD 700 to 1350) constructed extensive irrigation systems that diverted water from streams and rivers to their cacao orchards.[8] In the arid lands of the Yucatan, normally an inhospitable environment for cacao, the moist cenotes or sinkholes that dotted the karstic limestone terrain provided a humid microclimate for cacao gardens, free of pests and disease.[9] Several sixteenth-century chroniclers documented these geological formations. Diego de Landa observed that the Yucatec Maya had "sacred groves where they cultivate certain trees, like cacao."[10] According to Gaspar Antonio

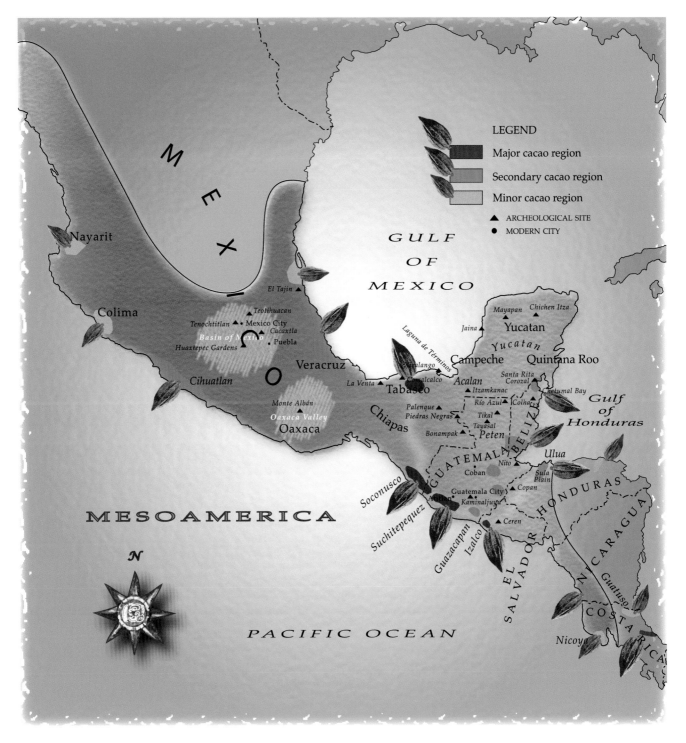

Figure 3.3   Cacao-growing regions.

Figure 3.4 A volcanic ash–covered young cacao tree from a Maya kitchen garden found at El Ceren, El Salvador, dating to the sixth century AD.

Chi, who described the customs in the Mayapan Saclac province of Yucatan, all lands were held in common except for "certain hollows and caves" and the plantations of fruit and cacao trees.[11] Those hollows were the cenotes that collected water, where cacao trees could thrive. Recent archaeological work in northeastern Yucatan has revealed stone walls surrounding dry cenotes that may have been the property boundaries of elites.[12]

At the opposite end of the scale, common people had house gardens that included cacao trees. The recently excavated village of Ceren, a small village in the center of what is now El Salvador, provides an extraordinary glimpse into personal house plots and the food grown by a community for their own use. Devastated by the volcanic eruption of Loma Caldera in about AD 590, the village was buried under fifteen feet of ash until rediscovered by accident, centuries later, by a bulldozer operator in 1978.[13] Not unlike Pompeii, the site is in a remarkable state of preservation, allowing archaeologists a rare firsthand assessment of the Cerenians' lifestyle. Evidence of the cultivation of many foods—maize, maguey, chilies, and *guayaba*, for instance—was found in small household gardens and adjacent milpas. But the garden plot at Household 4 revealed the most exciting surprise: a young cacao tree, with a developing flower attached to its trunk, whose ash-encased hollow form still stood in the ground (fig. 3.4). Inside the storeroom, four ceramic vessels contained cacao beans. One of them also had chili seeds, perhaps in preparation for a pre-Hispanic mole dish.[14]

journey by land and sea: cacao trade and trade centers

When did Mesoamericans begin cultivating and trading cacao? Although direct evidence is scant, chemical analyses have revealed that a sherd from a *tecomate* vessel dating to 1900–1500 BC from the Soconusco Pacific region of Chiapas (Structure 4, Mound 6, Paso de la Amada) once contained theobromine, a compound found in cacao. Another vessel, a deep bowl with cylindrical walls and a flat base (dating to 1650–1500 BC) from the Olmec site of El Manati on the gulf coast of Mexico, has also tested positive for cacao.[15] These, along with sherds from bowls, jars, and long-necked bottles with theobromine residue (dating to 1400–200 BC) from the lower Ulua Valley in northern Honduras, predate the earliest burial vessels (600–400 BC) that contained cacao from Colha, Belize (see fig. 4.9).[16] Thus, Mesoamericans have been cultivating and trading cacao since Early Preclassic times, possibly as early as 1900 BC.

A thousand years later, by the Classic period, an extensive trading network of overland, riverine, and sea routes had developed across Mesoamerica. Heightened demand for cacao and other luxury items generated a complex commercial structure fueled by Mexica (Valley of Mexico) and Maya merchants (fig. 3.5). Cacao-producing regions spawned ports of call, free-trade zones, and inland mercantile centers as merchants traveled to, from, or through them to exchange feathers, salt, jade, shells, obsidian, cotton, and other coveted items from faraway places for cacao.

Cacao brought great prosperity not only to the areas that grew it, such as Tabasco, but also to those provinces that had gained control over its trade and distribution. Santa Rita Corozal on Chetumal Bay along the Caribbean Sea in northern Belize is one example. It began as a small trading village as early as 300 BC and continued for over 1,200 years as a port for riverine and maritime trading. Strategically located on the Hondo and New rivers, it controlled access to both inland routes into the Peten and pan-American sea routes hugging the coast from Yucatan to the cacao-rich Ulua and Sula regions of Honduras.[17]

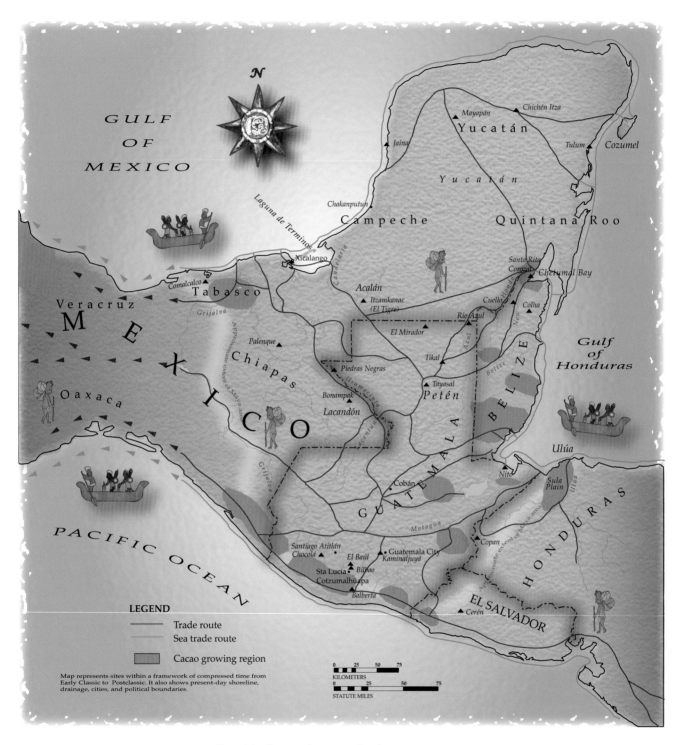

Figure 3.5   Cacao trade routes and trade centers.

During the long period of Santa Rita's commercial success, the monopolies over cacao trade held by numerous other regions flourished and died as political and military power shifts determined their prominence. The following examples of cacao monopolies reflect at least a thousand-year time span: Early Classic Teotihuacan in the Valley of Mexico; Cacaxtla, the Epiclassic capital of the Tlaxcalan region; and the Maya Chontal region of Acalan in Late Postclassic Campeche. Of the three, only Acalan was able to grow cacao, and this only in a limited amount.

TEOTIHUACAN

Archaeological evidence from Guatemala's southern piedmont along the Pacific coast strongly suggests that Teotihuacan had outposts in this cacao-rich land between AD 375 and 450. The foreign settlements most likely consisted of Teotihuacanos who were serving diplomatic, trade, or military missions far from their Mexican center.[18] Evidence from Balberta, Guatemala (an Early Classic period site), suggests such a liaison: green obsidian blades from Pachuca in Hidalgo, Mexico, were discovered in cached vessels along with ceramic or "counterfeit" cacao beans (see fig. 3.16). These caches perhaps exemplified the beginnings of a commercial relationship between Teotihuacan and the Pacific coast. Control over cacao and obsidian trade was certainly a strong incentive; perhaps this was initially achieved through overt military force by these Teotihuacan colonies before the resulting alliances occurred.[19]

Teotihuacan-style incensarios (censers) and cylindrical tripod vases with new hybrid artistic themes found in southern Guatemala bear further testimony to the vigorous commercial and cultural interchange between Teotihuacan and the Guatemalan Maya regions of Esquintla, Lago de Amatitlan, and even as far north as Tikal in the Peten region. Cacao imagery and Teotihuacano symbols are integrated on many of these vessels (see fig. 1.8), which reflect the eclectic, cosmopolitan mix of Teotihuacano, Maya, and Veracruz cultural styles that coalesced in southern Guatemala.

Censers from the Esquintla region often had butterfly deities or other Teotihuacan themes of warfare juxtaposed with cacao. The religious and militarist imagery of these incensarios (see fig. 4.10) reflected the ethos of merchants in a foreign land.[20] The most unusual and interesting censer from Esquintla with these Teotihuacano artistic and religious traits shows an anthropomorphic butterfly deity, emerging from a split, ripe cacao pod (fig. 3.6). A cacao pod forms the base of the lid. A watery "place," symbolic as the source of life, is in front on the base as well.

Figure 3.6   A butterfly deity emerging from a cacao pod. (Early Classic Maya censer from Esquintla, Guatemala)

Figure 3.7   A storm god impersonator with speech scrolls of cacao pods. (Early Classic mural, Techinantitla-Teotihuacan, Mexico)

Cultural exchange was by no means limited to the Guatemalan coastal area; imported Maya ceramics, eclectic murals with Maya-style art and writing, and locally produced "Mayoid" ceramics have been found throughout Teotihuacan apartment compounds.[21] For instance, the image on the vessel fragment found at Teotihuacan in figure 1.21 may be an idealized depiction of the southern piedmont in Chiapas and Guatemala: a blowgun hunter, a quetzal bird, and cacao trees set in a mountainous environment. On the west wall of the Techinantitla compound of Teotihuacan, a possible fertility ritual is taking place: two cacao pods are attached to the speech scroll of a storm god impersonator, suggesting that he is speaking of cacao, as he holds a lightning bolt in one hand and an offering in the other (fig. 3.7).[22]

CACAXTLA: "PLACE OF THE MERCHANT'S PACK"

The fall of Teotihuacan around AD 600 enabled small states to gain control over the trade corridors between the Basin of Mexico and the cacao regions in the Gulf Coast lowlands. One of these was Cacaxtla, a powerful hub for merchants within the Tlaxcalan region that reached its apogee between AD 650 and 900. Fifty miles southeast of Mexico City, it was the "Place of the Merchant's Pack"—as the term *cacaxtli* translates from Nahuatl—a toponym that indicates its superior role as a major trade center. Architectural and artistic elements at Cacaxtla reflect both Maya and Central Mexico stylistic influences.

A spectacularly painted fresco mural on the east stair wall of the sunken chamber known as Templo Rojo at Cacaxtla exemplifies the long-distance trade conducted during this period by armed *pochteca*-style merchants of Central Mexico. It is a rich composite of aquatic, agricultural, and fertility symbolism juxtaposed against commercial trading imagery (fig. 3.8). A water band that flows over the body of a snake frames the elaborate scene of a jade frog, a maize plant sprouting ears of tonsured Maya maize gods, a cacao tree, and the only monumental depiction of a lowland Maya deity outside the Maya zone: God L, the merchant god. Shrouded in his typical jaguar-skin attire and holding a blue walking stick, he stands before the fertile cacao tree laden with cacao pods on its trunk; a supernatural, winged-eyed quetzal bird flies above. God L's characteristic large hat is attached to his cacaxtli backpack; the hat morphs into his supernatural muan bird (screech owl) companion, who wears a "death eye" collar and has serpent-like attributes. The backpack holds quetzal feathers, a ball possibly of newly formed rubber from the latex sap of the rubber tree, and two containers perhaps of cacao beans, all products from the lowlands. The flint-bladed lance that props up the turtle carapace shield on his backpack reflects his role as the armed elite merchant.[23]

A closer look at God L proves that he is a deity: he has the Maya "god markings" on his arms and legs and the scroll eye of a Maya supernatural. Yet the Mixtec-style name glyph in front of him confirms that he is also a specifically named individual, "Four Dog." Perhaps this artistic blend of Mayan and Mixtec-Oaxacan traits was a way to legitimize a dynastic power based in mixed ancestry, while reinforcing claims to the profitable cacao trade between the lowland Maya areas and highland Mexico.[24]

ACALAN: "PLACE OF CANOES"

By the time of the Spanish conquest, the Maya in the Yucatan and adjoining regions along the Gulf of Mexico and the Caribbean had formed a powerful economic trading block, extending from western Tabasco to the Ulua River in northern Honduras.[25] The Yucatec Maya traded by overland routes to Tabasco and by sea in canoes to Ulua in Honduras and to Nicaragua. They carried their cloth, slaves, feathers, salt, knives, wax, copal, and other items to these regions and exchanged their goods for cacao and stone beads that they used as money.[26]

The first European explorer to glimpse this extensive trade network was evidently Christopher Columbus, during his fourth voyage to the New World in 1502.[27] He and his crew encountered an impressively large dugout trading canoe rowed by slaves off the coast of Honduras at Guanaja in the Bay Islands. It was loaded with people and goods—including bags of cacao beans—positioned underneath a thatched awning. Ferdinand, Christopher's son, later wrote an account of this encounter that underscored how valuable the cacao (called "almonds" by the Spaniards) must have been to the native traders, for "when any of these almonds fell, they all stooped to pick it up, as if an eye had fallen."[28]

One of the great centers of cacao trade within this economic block was the Chontal Maya province of Acalan—"Place of Canoes"—on the upper reaches of the Río Candelaria in what is now Campeche. The Chontal Maya of Acalan not only grew cacao but also maintained centuries of mercantile interaction throughout Mesoamerica. One of the temples at Itzamkanac, Acalan's remote capital, was dedicated to Ek Chuah, the Postclassic Maya merchant god (fig. 3.9). Sandwiched between Tabasco, the Peten area of Guatemala, and southwestern Yucatan, Acalan's location gave it considerable control over the extensive river system that flows into Laguna de Términos on the gulf coastline, as well as direct access to a major commercial center, Xicalango.[29] Acalan's tentacles also reached the town of Nito, an important outlet for nearby cacao-growing regions near the mouth of the Río Dulce in Guatemala. At the time of Cortés's arrival, Acalan's ruler, who was also the region's principal merchant, placed agents and created separate districts for his vassals and traders in Nito.[30]

Figure 3.8 (overleaf) The merchant god, with his pack, approaching a cacao tree and maize plant. (Late Classic mural, Cacaxtla, Mexico; © 2006 Bob Sacha)

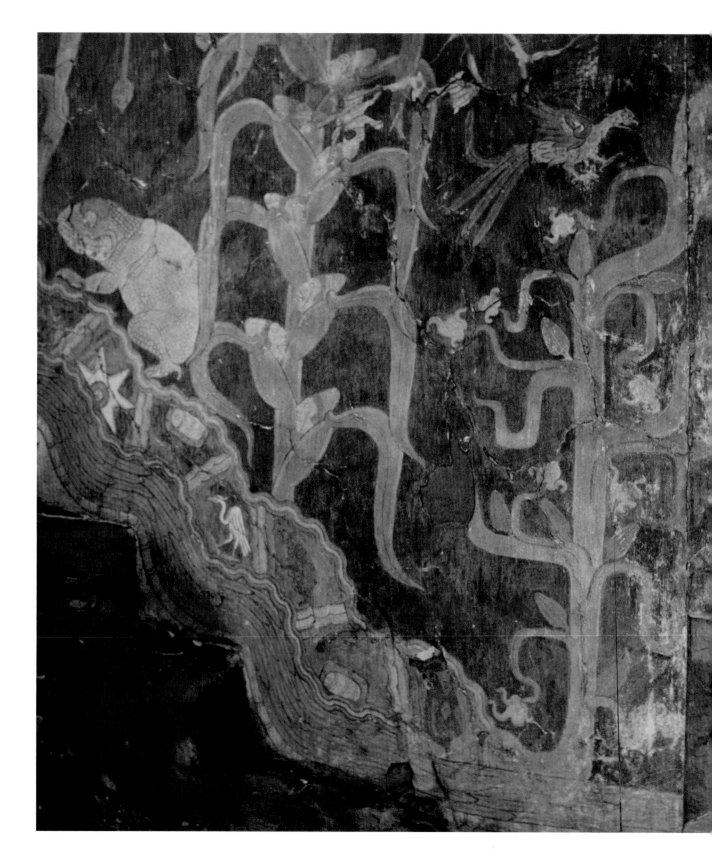

Figure 3.9   The merchant god Ek Chuah.
(Dresden Codex)

This appears to have been a common practice to strengthen control over the cacao trade. The lords of Tabasco's port of Xicalango likewise stationed agents in prominent cacao-producing areas. Southwest of Itzamkanac, Tayasal also depended on external exports and had outposts on the Caribbean coast to grow cacao, possibly at Nito or Chetumal. Much earlier, the lords of Chichen Itza during the Late Classic period had controlled a special port near Ascención Bay, the launching point for trade to Honduras for cacao, as well as other goods. The mural found at the Temple of the Warriors may depict such maritime activity (fig. 3.10). Mayapan, which replaced Chichen Itza's dominance after the fall of Chichen Itza around AD 1200, maintained economic ties to the Sula plain in Honduras, both for cacao and for the feathers for which it was renowned.[31]

Figure 3.10   A mural of village and maritime activity in the Temple of the Warriors in Chichen Itza, Mexico.

The Journey of cacao as Tribute

Rulers throughout Mesoamerica obtained cacao not only through trade but also as a form of tribute, a one-way mechanism, from subjugated peoples. From Maya overlords to Aztec kings, the quest for tribute was fueled by centuries of heightened mania for acquisitions of exotic goods. Some commodities, such as cacao, that were not essential to everyday living nevertheless helped those in power to maintain status through sumptuary display. This entrenched tribute system survived into colonial times and was eagerly adopted by the Spanish in the 1500s, as they co-opted the pre-Hispanic structure for their own gains.

Maya kings used tribute to support their royal households; wars, artisans, banquets, ritual festivals, building construction, and other necessities such as reciprocity obligations were financed by tribute payments. Scenes of presentations to the royal courts were often portrayed on polychrome vases in which Maya subjects kneel before their lords while offering platters of food in their outstretched hands; accompanying glyphs have been interpreted as tribute transactions.[32]

On one polychrome vessel, cacao appears as a possible tribute item or gift in a palace scene. In figure 3.11, a white bundle placed in front of the bench of the seated lord contains 24,000 cacao beans (three *pik*). Another striking presentation of cacao appears on one of several famous wall murals in the now-ruined three-room temple, Templo de las Pinturas, at Bonampak, located in the dense forest of Chiapas, Mexico. Vivid polychromatic renditions of Maya lords, dancers, musicians, warriors, and servants of the court, nearly life-size in stature, appear to be taking part in festive and ritual activities.

Five large white bundles placed in front of a royal throne are in a scene on the west wall in Room 1 (fig. 3.12a). Their contents remained a mystery until 1996, when infrared photography exposed the glyphs for "five pik kakaw" on one of them (fig. 3.12b).[33] Thus, each bundle contained roughly 40,000 cacao beans.[34] In front of the throne, a servant holds out a child, perhaps in a formal celebratory presentation of an heir to the court, while on a nearby wall, a procession of fourteen high-ranking lords wearing long white capes may have been invited guests; perhaps the cacao-filled bundles arrived with their entourages.[35] With confirmation that the white bags contained cacao beans, the scene became clearer: cacao was a critical part of this grand ritualized event.

Figure 3.11   A palace scene of tribute or the gift of a sack of cacao beans. (Late Classic Maya cylindrical vase)

Figure 3.12a A Bonampak mural showing a tribute scene. A palace ceremony with bags of cacao placed under the throne.

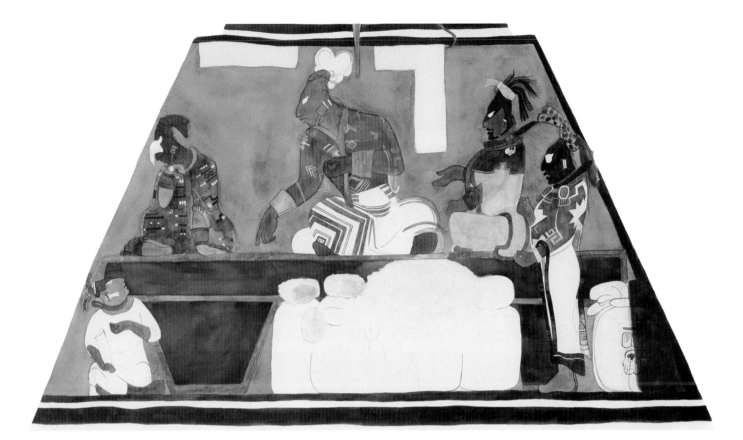

Figure 3.12b: A "5 pik kakaw" glyph on a bag of cacao beans in the Bonampak mural. (Room 1, West Wall, Templo de las Pinturas, Bonampak, Mexico; Late Classic Maya)

Tenochtitlan's Quest for Cacao: Journey of the Aztec Pochteca

Perhaps there is no better model for extracting cacao as tribute than what the imperial Aztecs of Tenochtitlan achieved through military expansion and subjugation. During its formative years in the fourteenth and fifteenth centuries, this great Aztec capital once ruled in close association with its sister community, Tlatelolco, whose ruins today, like those of Tenochtitlan, lie in the center of Mexico City. Although each had separate temples and rulers, Tenochtitlan evolved into a military power while Tlatelolco and its great marketplace established the empire's commercial footing, with principal merchants overseeing the expansion of trade.

Cacao first appeared within the Aztec provinces as a luxury trade item under Tlatelolco's last ruler, Moquihix.[36] When Tenochtitlan's new ruler Axayacatl slayed the defiant Moquihix, his warriors sacked Tlatelolco and took over the marketplace. Tlatelolco's merchants and people, placed under military rule, were then subjected to constant tribute. With the absorption of the commercial role of Tlatelolco, Tenochtitlan had solidified the linkage between Aztec military expansion and long-distance trading. The year was 1473, a year that may have launched the trajectory of long-distance trading for luxury goods by the Aztec merchant pochteca (fig. 3.13).[37] The association of the pochteca with the Aztec nobility and their role in religion and the expansionary policies of the Aztec state accorded them certain honor.[38] Their god was the long-nose god Yiacatecutli.[39] He was a manifestation of the Postclassic Maya's Ek Chuah, as he, too, had a Pinocchio-like nose and black face. In the Codex Féjérvary-Mayer, Yiacatecutli carries the symbol of the crossroads with merchants' footprints on them (fig. 3.14).

The chronicler Bernardino de Sahagún goes to great lengths to describe the four types of pochteca in sixteenth-century postconquest Mexico: the commanders of the pochteca; the slave traders, who were known as "bather of slaves"; the "royal travelers" or "vanguard" merchants, who carried out the bulk of the trade for the rulers and collected tribute; and the "disguised merchants." Members of this fourth group are of particular interest, for they were trader-spies sent out by Tenochtitlan's ruler to foreign territory in search of luxury goods, reconnoitering provinces before these were conquered. They entered enemy territory disguised as natives of that region to escape detection.[40] The stakes were high in this profession, because if caught, they would be killed and served up with chili sauce![41]

The conquest of the cacao-producing province of Soconusco by Tenochtitlan in 1500, largely attributed to these clever pochteca, dramatically increased the amount of

cacao paid as tribute to the Aztec power. The Aztec Codex Mendoza lists the five provinces located in the modern states of Guerrero, Chiapas, Oaxaca, Veracruz, and Puebla that paid tribute in cacao to the Aztec king Moctezuma. A page from this codex (fig. 3.15) depicts two bundles of cacao beside two jaguar skins; each bundle represents five loads of cacao, yielding ten loads in total. Soconusco in Chiapas paid the most: four hundred loads of cacao. With each load of cacao containing three *xipquipilli*, or 24,000 beans, a hefty weight of more than fifty pounds was borne on the backs of carriers.[42] If a subjugated province did not grow cacao, the cacao for the tribute payments had to be obtained elsewhere.

Figure 3.13 (left)   An Aztec pochteca merchant. (Codex Féjérvary-Mayer)

Figure 3.14 (right)   Yiacatecutli, the Aztec merchant god. (Codex Féjérvary-Mayer)

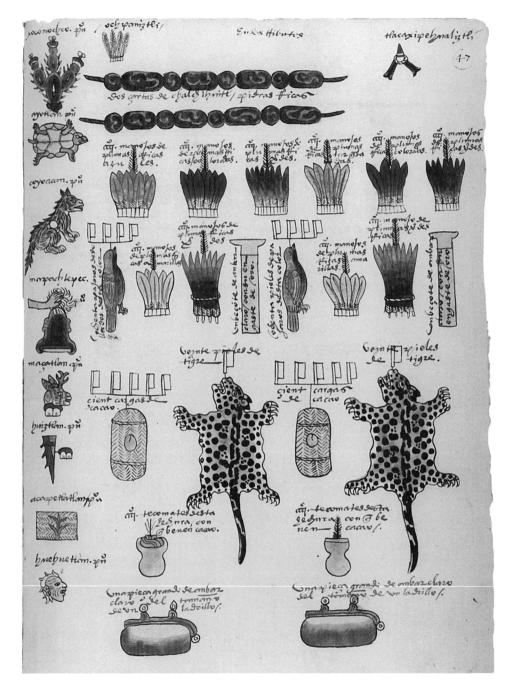

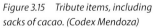

Figure 3.15   Tribute items, including sacks of cacao. (Codex Mendoza)

cacao: Money That Grows on Trees

Throughout the world, materials used in religious or social rites—as offerings, gifts, or bride price—often have acquired a standard of value, becoming money. This was certainly the case for cacao. As with other primitive currency, it was portable, durable, divisible, not easily counterfeited, and recognizable as a symbol for wealth.[43] Early in the sixteenth century, Oviedo y Valdés remarked with surprise that in Nicaragua most food and other essentials in the markets—including wives, slaves, and prostitutes (which were the same price as a rabbit)—could be bought with cacao beans: "They guard them and hold them in the same price and esteem as the Christians hold gold or coin; because these almonds are regarded as such by them, as they can buy all things with them. In the way . . . a rabbit is worth ten of these almonds . . . and a slave costs one hundred almonds, more or less."[44]

Money may have grown on trees, but the mechanisms that determined which cacao varieties were to be consumed and which were to be reserved for money are still enigmatic. In its role as money, cacao may have been limited at first to one special variety but over time came to include all varieties. Size may have been a factor, too; the smaller beans were reputed to have been the most flavorful for drinking, so the larger, less-flavorful varieties may have held up better as hand-to-hand currency.[45]

As with any other medium used as money, attempts to counterfeit cacao beans occurred frequently. The counterfeiter had to be quite skilled in his craft, for falsification would have been a tedious task: each delicate bean had to be cut open and the skin then resealed after the edible nib was removed and the space refilled with dirt. The handiwork had to be good enough to fool most people. "To guard against this fraud, he who receives them goes through them one by one when he counts them, and places his index finger against his thumb, pressing each one. Although the counterfeit one be packed tight it can be felt to the touch not to be as firm as the real one."[46]

Perhaps even the gods were fooled by the unusual counterfeited cacao beans found at Balberta, a site in the Cotzumalhuapa area of western Guatemala (fig. 3.16). More than four hundred fake cacao beans fashioned from local clays had been placed inside four dedicatory cache vessels for the main pyramid when it was built. Also included in the caches were valuable green obsidian artifacts from the Pachuca source of highland Mexico, an indication that the vessels' contents were highly coveted. The counterfeiter's talent was remarkable: many of the beans duplicated unique irregularities representative of known morphological differences in *criollo* varieties.[47] Whether the bean

Figure 3.16 *An Early Classic cache of fake cacao bean clay effigies (bottom) and actual cacao beans (top). (Balberta, Guatemala)*

effigies were merely symbolic or truly meant to fool the gods, their placement inside the buried caches within this ancient time capsule ensured their permanency.

The Demise of the Pochteca and Cacao Production: The Spanish Conquest

Although cacao continued to be used as money well into at least the nineteenth century, the Spanish entry into the New World turned the world of cacao and trade upside down. Local markets still operated, but with the fall of Tenochtitlan, the pochteca's supremacy was eradicated within five years after the conquest. The repercussions on indigenous commerce, cacao production, and overall economy throughout Mesoamerica were devastating.

Acalan, the great trading power within the Yucatan economic block, lost its supremacy in cacao trade within thirty years. The introduction of European diseases such as smallpox and Spanish exploitation of the native population, together with the economic and commercial disruption with trading entities such as Tabasco and Honduras, ruined Acalan. Its population shrank to four thousand Chontal Maya by 1553 from an estimated minimum of ten thousand in 1530. The coup de grace, however, occurred in 1557, when the Spanish authorities, finding the remaining Chontal population centered in the Candelaria Basin too remote for Franciscan conversion efforts, moved the Chontal Maya—some carried away in chains—to the new site of Tixchel near Laguna de Términos along the gulf coast. The cacao trees were cut down, along with copal trees, to discourage further resistance to the move.[48]

Perhaps the most poignant story within the geopolitical history of sacred cacao groves occurred in the Pacific coastal province of Suchitepequez in what is now Guatemala. Suchitepequez and the adjacent region of Soconusco in today's Chiapas, both known for their superior criollo cacao, were characterized by a long, pre-Hispanic history of internal warring over their rich cacao lands.[49] In addition, Aztec control of the Soconusco cacao region before 1500 threatened Maya control of cacao in the Suchitepequez province, adding further regional strife.[50]

Such were the dynamics that defined the year of 1522, when Tz'utujil messengers from the coastal town of Xeoj went to Cortés in Mexico and, presenting him with eight loads of cacao, enlisted his aid to settle a border dispute with the Quiché.[51] Little did they know that this plea would open the door to their ultimate destruction, for Cortés sent as his captain the cruel and greedy Pedro de Alvarado, one who had earlier ordered the ransacking of Moctezuma's warehouse of cacao in Tenochtitlan. Alvarado settled the dispute but also demanded cacao as tribute, from the spring of 1524 until his death in 1541, collecting from his *encomienda* of Atitlan, Guatemala, 1,400 *xiquipillis* of cacao a year, or 11,200,000 *nibs*. In the meantime, he had cut a wide swath of enslavement and disease, turning the wealthy Tz'utujil kingdom inside out.[52] Throughout the eighteenth century, with most of the cacao lands in Spanish ownership in Suchitepequez, lack of a proper workforce and the encroachment of cattle-raising haciendas exacerbated a downward spiral of cacao production.

By the middle of the nineteenth century, coffee had replaced cacao as the major crop within the Pacific piedmont.[53] As a final act of irony, the remaining cacao trees in the Suchitepequez region were cut to the ground as timber for railroad ties for the construction of rail lines that would bear trainloads of coffee. The sacred cacao groves of the tropical forests of the Pacific piedmont virtually disappeared.[54] Today, where stone monuments depicting jaguars and ballplayers with cacao and cacao offerings still dot the fields of El Baúl and Bilbao, the cacao trees that inspired this monumental art no longer flourish.

serve up the chocolate:
Drinks, vessels, and Glyphs

Then, in his house, the ruler was served his chocolate, with which he finished [his repast]—green, made of tender cacao; honeyed chocolate made with ground-up dried flowers—with green vanilla pods; bright red chocolate; orange-colored chocolate; rose-colored chocolate; black chocolate; white chocolate.

The chocolate was served in a painted gourd vessel, with a stopper also painted with a design, and [having] a beater; or in a painted gourd, smoky [in color], from neighboring lands, with a gourd stopper, and a jar rest of ocelot skin or of cured leather. In a small net were kept the earthen jars, the strainer with which was purified the chocolate, a large earthen jar for making the chocolate.   Bernardino de Sahagún, ca. 1550

The world's first chocolate treat was the Mesoamerican cacao drink. Whether as the frothed kakaw beverage of the Maya or the foaming *cacahuatl* drink of the Aztecs, it was a labor-intensive endeavor that began with the domestication, cultivation, and harvesting of the cacao tree. Processing the cacao bean into pure chocolate, a Maya achievement, was perfected with chemistry-like precision. The resulting cacao drink required special ceramic vessels, designated solely for its consumption, that were often embedded with mythological, sociopolitical, and cosmological histories.

It is not hard to imagine, then, why the cacao seed and tree became a sacred entity to pre-Columbian cultures; the enormous effort necessary for just one cup of cacao drink demanded an almost religious commitment. No wonder the drink acquired elite status during ritual and feasting events, as the beverage of choice for the gods.

Preparation and culinary secrets: The Drink

The basic method of processing raw cacao beans into chocolate has changed little in thirty-five hundred years in Mexico and Central America. Despite the growing commercialization of chocolate by many modern *cacaoteros* in Oaxaca, Tabasco, and other regions who use gas-fired roasters and mechanized stone grinders, the process

Figure 4.1 Processing cacao: a (above left), cacao pods piled on the ground; b (above right), extracting cacao beans from pods.

remains a home-based, hands-on endeavor in less-urban areas, where the age-old traditional methods described here are still in use (fig. 4.1a–f).

Once extracted from the cacao pod, the beans (which are actually seeds) are dumped into bins or containers, where they ferment in their sugary pulp for approximately three days. During fermentation, they undergo a complex chemical transformation through which they lose most of their acidic properties. The fermented beans are laid out to dry in the hot tropical sun. As the beans are finally roasted over a hot fire on the terra-cotta surface of the *comal*, they release one of the most aromatic smells known to mankind. After their paper-thin husks are removed, the roasted beans are ground repeatedly on a stone metate with a stone mano—sometimes over a fire to hasten the process—until they are transformed into a smooth, gleaming, fatty, semiliquid paste. This is chocolate in its truest form, with the cacao butter still intact. If not used immediately, the paste can be shaped into small balls or patties, ready to use when needed. Each pod contains enough cacao beans to produce about seven cups of chocolate, or two dark chocolate bars for the modern chocoholic.

This New World drink took on different colors, textures, and tastes as the ancient chocolate connoisseur enhanced it with a wide range of ingredients and flavors. We know from several sixteenth-century historical accounts that the original cacao drink of tepid water and cacao paste was a bitter concoction, the bitterness often heightened with the addition of chilies.[1] It was frequently mixed with roasted maize or soft maize dough.

Figure 4.1, continued   Processing cacao:
c (top left), a bin of fermenting beans;
d (top right), drying cacao beans; e (above),
roasting cacao beans over a hot comal;
f (right), grinding cacao beans on a metate.

The Aztecs, Mixtecs, Maya, and others also ground and mixed with the cacao paste a variety of flowers and seeds from trees, plants, and vines that thrived in the same tropical rainforest environment as the cacao tree. This included strongly aromatic flowers that grew on trees, such as the sacred earflower (*Cymbopetalum penduliflorum*), the heart flower (*Talauma mexicana*), the white "popcorn" flower (*Bourreria formosa*), or the "flor de cacao" (*Quararibea funebris*), all of which gave the drink a taste similar to black pepper, curry, or anise (see figs. 2.19, 5.9, and 5.6). Other rainforest ingredients spicing the original chocolate drink were vanilla pods from the orchid *Vanilla planifolia* (see fig. 5.10), achiote from the annatto bush (*Bixa orellana*)—which gave the drink its blood-red color—and seeds from the sapote or mamey tree (*Calocarpum mammosum*) and the sacred ceiba or silk-cotton tree (*Ceiba pentandra*). The Mexican pepper leaf or root beer plant (*Piper sanctum*), the allspice berry (*Pimenta dioica*), and liquid from the bark of the rubber tree (*Castilla elastica*) were also ingredients. If sweetened, this was done sparingly with honey or syrup from the maguey plant.

The Foam: window to the soul

The most essential and sacred part of the ritual cacao drink was the foam on top. Indeed, the ancient Zapotecs believed that the vital force of the wind god Pée was present in everything, even in the animated foam of chocolate. Contemporary folklore still holds that "chocolate is for the body, but the foam is for the soul." Not surprisingly, vessels of foaming chocolate appear in ceremonial, palace, and feasting scenes depicted on Maya Classic period ceramics and in Mixtec codices (see figs. 2.19, 2.20, and 2.26). A food riddle from the Maya *Book of Chilam Balam of Chumayel* describes the red foam colored by achiote in allegorical terms, comparing it to the crests of cardinals.[2]

We even know how the foam was initially "raised," a task that seems to have always been delegated as woman's work. In the Mexican Tudela Codex and on at least one Maya vase, women stand and pour chocolate from one vase to another until foam appears (fig. 4.2 and 4.3). Stirring sticks and spoons were also used for this purpose before the Spanish wooden *molinillo*, an elongated paddle with movable rings, was introduced to create the foam with an easy twirl. In addition, certain foaming agents added to the chocolate drink produced a frothing: the flor de cacao (*Quararibea funebris*) and sugir (used by the Lacandon Maya), to name a few. Often the foam was removed and stored for later use. Contemporary Lacandon Maya in eastern Chiapas spoon the

Figure 4.2   An Aztec woman pouring chocolate from a standing position to raise the foam. (Tudela Codex)

Figure 4.3   A woman pouring chocolate from a standing position. Detail from figure 3.2. (Late Classic Maya cylinder vase)

Figure 4.4 Burying pataxte (Theobroma bicolor): a (top left), buried beans; b (top right), a Zapotec woman burying the beans; c (right), white, calcified beans at a market in Zaachila, Oaxaca, Mexico.

foam off and place it on top of maize gruel, to be gobbled up.[3] To them and many other Mesoamericans, cacao foam is the most desirable part.

Women in the rural Oaxaca Valley still go to great lengths to continue the tradition of foam. There, a secretive process is passed down from generation to generation among women. They bury pataxte beans (*Theobroma bicolor*) within layers of soil and mats in the ground, watering them for six full moons. The result is a calcified, powdery-white bean called *cacao blanco* (fig. 4.4). When ground and mixed with regional chocolate *atole* drinks, these expensive beans create a bodacious head of foam. Even today, the value of a rural Mexican woman is often measured by the amount of foam she can produce on chocolate.

Humble origins: The ever-evolving vessel for chocolate

As sacred containers that housed a sacred food, vessels for chocolate are a distinctive element within the ceramic traditions of Mesoamerica. All cultures throughout Mexico and Central America contributed to the rich corpus of chocolate vessels, cups, and pots. But the aesthetic sensitivity of pre-Columbian Maya chocolate vessels can be especially breathtaking, often challenging the artistic superiority of their ceramic counterparts from more-well-known ancient civilizations. During its 2,500-year evolution, the Maya chocolate vessel gave us glyphic text of chocolate "recipes" and perhaps even changed form to accommodate the all-important foam.

The sixteenth-century Aztec ruler Moctezuma may very well have drunk his chocolate from golden cups—as one early Spanish chronicler had testified with awe—but the first vessels for chocolate (as is true of all Mesoamerican containers) were most likely made from simple natural objects, such as gourds and calabashes, or vegetal material such as wood.[4] Although such highly perishable items have not survived, our evidence for such speculation lies mainly with Classic period ceramics, which in a way try to recall these humble beginnings. Many are not only gourdlike or calabash-like in shape (fig. 4.5) but also have glyphic texts on their surfaces that describe them as "thin-gourd-like," even when they may not be necessarily thin. Other Classic period ceramic vessels have not only glyphic text but also surface treatment suggesting that the original vessel was made of wood (fig. 4.6). The text on the cylinder vase in figure 4.7 refers to a type of thin-walled gourd still used by the Chol and Tzotzil Maya, a *tsimal hay*.[5] The colorful scene includes drug consumption and the use of enemas to induce hallucinations. Itzamna, the creator god, oversees the preparation for the ceremony from inside his cave, perhaps with a large cup of chocolate in front of him.

Figure 4.5   Maya glyphs for "frothy cacao" on an Early Classic bowl from the Naranjo, Guatemala, area.

Opposite:

Figure 4.6 (above)   A vessel intended for cacao. It has been painted to resemble wood. (Late Classic Maya)

Figure 4.7 (below)   A glyphic text (in glyph band, upper left) on a vessel referring to a certain thin-walled gourd, tsimal hay. Itzamna is on the far left in a cave. (Late Classic Maya cylindrical vase)

Figure 4.8 (left)   A long-necked ceramic bottle of the same type as one that contained a cacao drink, perhaps of fermented cacao pulp. (Early Preclassic, Ulua Valley, Honduras)

Figure 4.9 (right)   A Preclassic Maya spouted vessel from Colha, Belize, that contained chocolate.

Preclassic spouted pots: where's the foam?

The earliest examples of ceramics that held chocolate and cacao were simple bowl and calabash forms (or tecomates) found in the Pacific coastal regions of Chiapas and in the gulf coastal region of Tabasco. However, as a general rule, from the Early Preclassic through the Early Classic, they are more likely to have been made with spouts, curved surfaces, doubled angled or highly flared walls, and a monochromatic surface treatment, lacking the polychromatic vigor that later evolved.[6]

The long-necked spout vessel from the Ulua Valley in northern Honduras (dating to 1400–1100 BC) is an Early Preclassic spouted ceramic form; it may have contained an alcoholic drink of fermented cacao pulp (fig. 4.8).[7] The spouted, stirrup "chocolate pots" dating to 600–400 BC from the Maya site of Colha in northern Belize (fig.

Chapter Four

4.9) are also early examples of ceramics that once contained chocolate. Their spouts, handles, and curved surfaces not only discouraged the effusive artist expression that later defined Maya vases but also bring up the question of how their owners could have prepared frothed, foaming chocolate in them.

The small openings and intruding handles on these Colha spouted vessels would have made frothing difficult for even the most industrious pre-Columbian woman. Chocolate could not have been poured back and forth or easily beaten with a stirring instrument. Researchers have suggested that the Preclassic Maya were not yet foaming their chocolate.

Around AD 400 during the Early Classic period, the manufacturing of spouted vessels in the Maya area radically declined at approximately the same time that Teotihuacano settlers infiltrated the Pacific coastal cacao-growing region of Soconusco. With their occupation, the Teotihuacan cylinder-shaped tripod vases influenced Maya ceramic production and perhaps accommodated an alternative method of preparing chocolate.[8] The shape of these vases could easily accommodate the back-and-forth pouring method to produce foam. The Maya incised vessel with Tlaloc (a highland Mexico rain god) and cacao tree imagery in figure 4.10 is most likely a product of this vessel evolution. Its Esquintla-style execution places its origin within the Maya Pacific region.

Tlaloc imagery and pyramids with the distinct Teotihuacan architectural style (referred to as *talud-tablero*) appear on another spectacular tripod vessel discovered at the fifth-century Margarita tomb at Copan, Honduras, the tomb of Copan's founder, Yax K'uk Mo'. Appropriately nicknamed "the Dazzler" (fig. 4.11), this polychromatic stuccoed vessel contained a dark layer of residue, which was confirmed as chocolate at the Hershey Laboratories in Pennsylvania.[9]

Figure 4.10   Rain gods and cacao trees on a Teotihuacan-influenced vessel. (Early Classic Maya incised tripod vase from Esquintla, Guatemala, with normal [top] and rollout [bottom] views)

Figure 4.11 (opposite)   A vessel that contained chocolate, nicknamed "The Dazzler." (Early Classic Maya tripod vessel from Copan, Honduras)

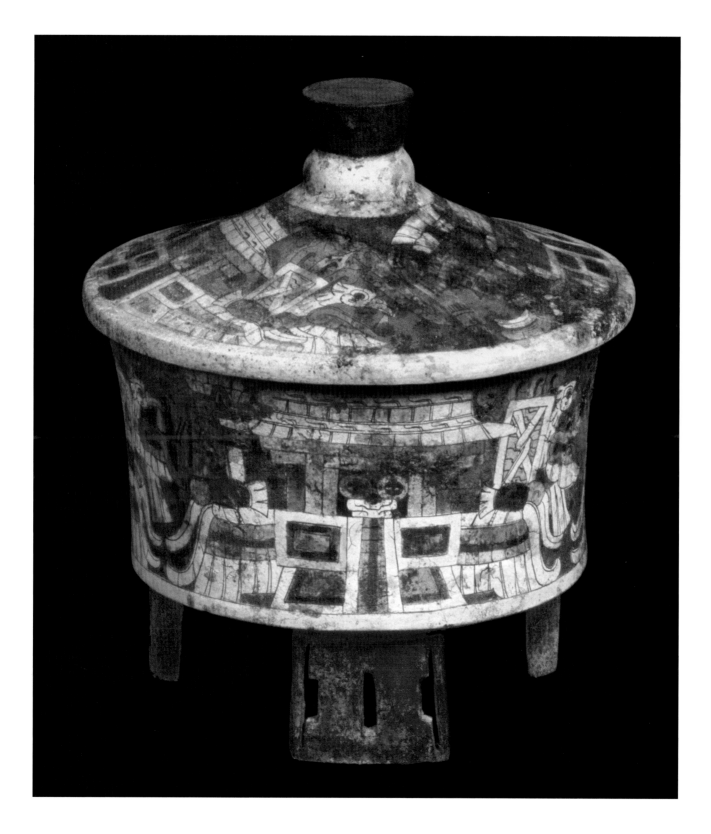

Came into being   was blessed   its surface   its writing   his drinking vessel his food frothy

Figure 4.12   A glyphic example of the Primary Standard Sequence (rollout view of fig. 4.23).

classic period exuberance: polychrome, glyphs, and artists

Beginning around AD 400, there was an explosion of wealth and a resulting proliferation of trade items. Ceramics for chocolate were used not only as serving vessels for the elites but also as ritual regal gifts and funeral objects found in the tombs of elite, and sometimes non-elite, individuals. They sometimes were part of serving sets. To meet the demands of growing affluence, and perhaps serving as a kind of one-upmanship in elite society, elaborate scenes of palace, cosmological, and historic events started to appear on Maya ceramics, including those used for cacao. This pictorial elaboration required flatter surfaces and simpler shapes. Maya chocolate vessels had three general shapes: cylinder vases, bowls and dishes, and plates. The cylinder vases, bowls, and dishes were called "drinking vessels," or *uch'ab*, while the plates were designated as *lak*. They all could contain liquid foods: primarily chocolate and drinks made with ground-up corn called *ul* (today's atole).[10]

Besides the simplification of form and the appearance of three classes of shape, another important development occurred: the Maya writing system, carved and painted on stone and frescoed surfaces at Maya sites, began to appear on the surface

| cacao | lineage member | youth | child of woman | (name) | holy | (name) | child of man |

of all three vessel shapes during the Classic period. These hieroglyphics record the type of vessel (cup, plate, etc.), the patron it was made for, the type of food the vessel was to contain, and sometimes the artist's name (fig. 4.12). Known as the Primary Standard Sequence (PSS) among Mayanists, this dedicatory formula was scribed onto many Classic period Maya vessels, revealing not only the actual glyph for cacao and its many variations (fig. 4.13) but also the various descriptions, the so-called recipes, for cacao drinks of the ancient Maya:[11]

iximte'el kakaw	"maize tree" cacao
y-utal kakaw	"sustenance" cacao
tshih te'el kakaw	"tree-fresh" cacao
tsih [kakaw]	"fresh" (cacao)
te'kakaw	"tree" cacao
k'ab kakaw	"juice" cacao (using honey)
om kakaw	"frothy" or "foaming" cacao

Figure 4.13a   Cacao glyph variations from codices and vessels: fish head variant ka.

Figure 4.13b   Cacao glyph variations from codices and vessels: fish head variant ka *with suffix* wa *by a scribe named Ah Maxam.*

Figure 4.13c   Cacao glyph variations from codices and vessels: comb ka *and fish head variant with two dots for repetitive pronunciation of the* ka *syllable.*

Figure 4.13d   Postclassic horizontal double-comb variant, ka-ka, with suffix wa.

Figure 4.14   Glyphic text (upper glyph band, right half) indicating that the vessel is for "tree fresh cacao pulp." (Late Classic Maya cylindrical vase from Campeche, Mexico)

CYLINDER DRINKING VASES

On some cylindrical vases, the pictorial scene is one continuous story. The palace scene on the vase from Campeche (AD 600–750) in figure 4.14 depicts a meeting between the Hero Twins and the Underworld god Itzamna. The severed head of perhaps the twins' father (the maize god) stares intently at Itzamna. Large glyphs encircle the rim and also appear as "structural" components of the building piers. The glyphic inscriptions tell us that the vessel is for "tree-fresh" cacao pulp, a deliciously sweet, gelatinous substance surrounding the seeds that is still enjoyed today (fig. 4.15). On others, such as the cylinder vase of figure 4.6, the surface is divided into two halves with an obverse and reverse image of the same scene on each side. The cacao glyph appearing in the dedicatory formula along the rim indicates that this vessel's intended use was for cacao.

The style of cylindrical cacao vessels varied considerably as one approached the southern extremities of the Maya region in Honduras, El Salvador, as well as in Costa Rica. The cacao vessels discovered buried under volcanic ash of the seventh century at the site of Ceren, El Salvador, for instance, lack the glyphic presence but maintain the vibrant polychromatic scenes of those produced by their northern Maya neighbors (fig. 4.16).

The carved, white marble vases linked to cacao drinking from the cacao-rich Ulua district of Honduras pose an even more striking variation.[12] Most are either tall cylindrical vessels or shorter tripod vessels that may reflect the earlier tradition of

Figure 4.15   A girl eating cacao pulp.

Teotihuacan tripod influence. Most also have two carved handles of animal forms, ranging in species from monkeys, snakes, and bats to birds, felines, and an unidentified crested animal.[13] Some have tripod feet; others rest on a ring base. Remaining pigment fragments still evident on the exteriors of many indicate that these finely carved marble vases had once been covered with red pigment or red or blue/green stucco, perhaps for certain ceremonial purposes. Only a corpus of approximately two hundred vases or fragments of this type are known to exist in museum and private collections today. However, they once were traded widely across Mesoamerica along with cacao from the Ulua Valley within elite circles, reflecting a long tradition of marble vase production from this cacao-growing region since Early Classic times. The vessel in figure 4.17 with jaguar handles has the prominent carved scroll pattern characteristic of these vessels. Deity heads appear on either side.[14]

Figure 4.16 (left)   A vessel from Ceren, El Salvador. (Late Classic Maya vase)

Figure 4.17 (right)   A carved marble vessel with jaguar handles from a cacao-growing region, widely traded along with cacao. The prominent scroll pattern is characteristic of these vessels. (Late Classic Maya vase from Ulua, Honduras)

Figure 4.18   A long-legged tripod vessel from Costa Rica with characteristic saurian legs. It has burn marks on the body, suggesting that the drink was heated.

Meanwhile, the secondary cacao-growing region of Costa Rica was creating its own form of cacao drinking vessels. Beginning as early as AD 100, one common form that arose within the Atlantic Watershed zone was a long-legged tripod vessel with a globular body and small flared mouth. This type of vessel may have been used frequently in funeral ceremonies. Carbonized burn marks at the base suggest that perhaps the drink was heated. The tripod supports took the form of various animals, including reptilian or effigy figures. The example in figure 4.18, dating to AD 100–500, has lizard or saurian creatures on its legs and obvious burn marks.

Classic period Mixtec tripod ollas from the Oaxaca Valley are reminiscent of this Costa Rica style. They, along with the wider-rimmed tripod *cajetes*, are depicted as vessels for ritual drinks such as pulque and chocolate in Mixtec codices (see fig. 2.20).

PLATES

In many tombs, plates (*laks*) are often found stacked like dishes, and in some instances, a vase or bowl would be placed on top, suggesting that the plate itself might be the offering.[15] But they were also containers for sacrificial offerings; although glyphs on Maya plates are less likely than those of vases to reveal their contents, a few were specifically designated for cacao. The text of a tripod plate from Homul in Guatemala (fig. 4.19) records that it contained "tree-fresh cacao," most likely the gelatinous pulp inside the pod. The PSS glyphs on another plate (fig. 4.20) translate as "his drinking vessel for his food cacao."[16]

Plates lacking a glyphic description of their contents have tested positive for cacao residue at the Hershey Laboratory. Two such examples from the Sub-Jaguar tomb at Copan, Honduras, include a "tamale" platter or plate and a vessel that contained cacao with fish bones.[17] Could these be the remains of an early mole-like sauce?

Figure 4.19   Glyphs (not visible) suggest that this three-legged plate was for "tree-fresh cacao," the thick, gelatinous pulp of the cacao pod. A dancer on its interior bottom surface and cormorants on the interior and exterior walls are common themes of the Homul style. (Late Classic polychrome plate from Homul, Guatemala)

Figure 4.20   A waterlily deity and glyphs that read "his drinking vessel for his food cacao." (Late Classic Maya polychrome plate)

Figure 4.21   A palace scene showing a tripod serving plate of tamales topped with what may be mole-like sauce, under the raised dais in the center of the scene. (Late Classic Maya cylindrical vase)

We experience mole today as a sauce prepared with chocolate and a variety of chilies, nuts, and other ingredients (depending on the type of sauce and regional variations) poured over meats, fowl, and even tamales. Historical folklore has claimed that the sixteenth-century colonial Spanish in Mexico were the creators of this ingenious culinary sauce. But archaeological and ceramic findings seem to suggest otherwise. Such a sauce may well have been a pre-Hispanic delight since at least AD 600. In fact, platters or plates of tamales coated with a chocolate-colored sauce appear in several palace scenes on Maya cacao vases (fig. 4.21, underneath the dais; fig. 2.19, below the dais to the right). And in a storehouse under the volcanic ash of Ceren, El Salvador, a vessel was found that contained cacao separated from chili peppers by a layer of cotton gauze—preparation as if for a pre-Columbian mole sauce.[18]

BOWLS

Bowls or cups that contained cacao varied considerably in appearance, shape, and form. The bowl-like vessel in figure 4.22 from the Yucatan is an unusual Early Classic receptacle emulating a squash. The large-head-variant glyphs in each of its segments tell us that it was to serve "*b'ukuts* cacao" (*bu-ku-tsi ka-ka-wa*). What this was is unclear, but surely it was for the gods, because it also appears in the Dresden Codex as an offering to the rain god Chac.[19] On another Classic bowl (figs. 4.12 and 4.23), the fishlike cacao glyph in the rim PSS text and in the middle of the vertical column of glyphs appears with bubbles in front of its head, a symbol for frothy cacao.

One of the most beautifully shaped bowls is an effigy deer vessel (fig. 4.24) from the tomb of Copan's founding king. It contained not only a sizable piece of cacao but also a cacao-stained shell, perhaps an instrument to scoop cacao from the bowl.[20] Another unusual vessel (fig. 4.25), a thin-walled lidded bowl from the Alta Verapaz region of Guatemala, has a molded figure of a supernatural persona atop the lid; its glyphic text states that the bowl was for cacao.[21]

Opposite:

Figure 4.22 (upper left)   A squash-shaped bowl with the bu-ku-tsi ka-ka-wa *glyph. (Early Classic bowl from Yucatan, Mexico)*

Figure 4.23 (upper right)   "Frothy" cacao glyph, the middle glyph in the vertical glyphic text on right. See also figure 4.12 upper rim text. (Late Classic Maya polychrome bowl)

Figure 4.24 (lower left)   A Late Classic Maya effigy deer vessel found with cacao residue inside in a tomb in Structure 16 at Copan in Honduras.

Figure 4.25 (lower right)   The glyphic text on the lid (last glyph on right) indicates that the bowl was for cacao. (Late Classic Maya lidded bowl)

Figure 4.26 The signature glyph of the artist Ah Maxam appears in the glyphic text around the base, ninth from the left. (Late Classic Maya, from Naranjo, Guatemala)

THE ARTISTS

As chocolate vessels became a highly desirable commodity of trade during the Classic period, a whole class of scribes and painters, often of royal and noble lineage, evolved. Members of this stratum of elite Maya and Aztec society were not only professionally trained in workshops and schools in the arts of painting, writing, and astronomy but also, in the case of the Maya, often signed their work. For example, the artist-scribe Ah Maxam signed three known cylinder vases for cacao. On one (fig. 4.26), the glyphic text states that he was "son of holy king of Naranjo."[22] On another cacao vessel from a tomb at Ek Balam, a Late Classic site in the Maya lowlands, an even more elaborate text states that the artist was "the Warrior who Cuts Hearts, the Handsome One, Head/Prince of the Earth, sacred king of Taloi."[23]

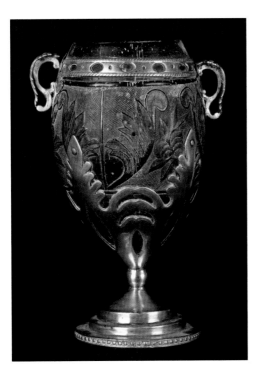

Figure 4.27   An incised coconut-husk chocolate cup with silver supports. (Colonial period)

The Modern Chocolate Vessel and Drink

The conquering Spanish culture continued the tradition of the chocolate pot and vessels, as the Spaniards absorbed the Mesoamericans' love of chocolate. The long tradition of the gourd, calabash, and other natural materials was reinvented by European aesthetics of elaborately carved scenes and silver supports (fig. 4.27). Ceramics of the sixteenth, seventeenth, and eighteenth centuries also reflected a more European sensibility (fig. 4.28), as did the china and silver chocolate pots that came to be coveted in colonial Spanish America. Chocolate vessels in Mesoamerica today vary in shape and artistic complexity but have a far different appearance than their pre-Columbian predecessors (figs. 4.29 and 4.30). Only the humble calabash (*jicara*) vessel designated for chocolate has survived through nearly four millennia of changes. Whether plain, incised and burned, carved, or highly lacquered with a polychromatic vibrancy, this vessel has retained its prominence in the ritual of drinking chocolate throughout Central America and Mexico (fig. 4.31).

The pre-Columbian cacao beverage with its potpourri of additives also changed. While it evolved into the specialties one finds today throughout Mesoamerica—such as atole, *champurrado, tejate, batido, tisté,* and *chorrote* (pozol)—it did so with many different ingredients.

Figure 4.28 Majolica ware: (above) a chocolate jar originally from the Convento de Santo Domingo, La Antigua, Guatemala, dated to the eighteenth century; (left) a chocolate cup originally from Beatrio de Indias del Rosario, La Antigua, Guatemala, dated to the eighteenth century.

Figure 4.29   A contemporary chocolate pot and cup from a serving set, from Jalisco, Mexico.

Figure 4.30 A contemporary chocolate pot and molinillo from Michoacán, Mexico.

Figure 4.31   Contemporary painted calabash cups for chocolate, from Coban, Guatemala.

As the European and native cultures merged with one another more than five hundred years ago, imported spices and condiments from the Old World—cinnamon, anise, black pepper, sesame seeds, and almonds—replaced many of the original flavorings once extracted from rainforest flowers and seeds. Wheat and rice also became part of this new hybrid chocolate drink in addition to, or in place of, maize. But the sixteenth-century European palate for sweetness imposed the most dramatic transformation. For when sugar was added to the bitter but sacred drink of the Maya, this beverage from the New World tropical forests came to belong to the rest of the world.

The Healing Powers of chocolate: Folk Medicine, Nutrition, and Pharmacology

Cast ye the needful with the paraphernalia ye four gods. Ye four Bacabs. Cast it into the slightly soured atole. Remove it all into the opening of his harsh breathing. When it enters into the opening, cast in the virgin cacao. *The Ritual of the Bacabs*

The therapeutic and nutritional properties of cacao have been at the forefront of human knowledge since remote antiquity. The Maya, Aztecs, and other Mexica peoples transformed every manifestation of the cacao tree—the seed, leaf, bark, oil (or butter), and flower—into effective curatives. Cacao was used not only by itself as the primary healing agent but also as a vehicle for other medicinal plant compounds that were mixed with it. The native peoples' formulas were eagerly adopted and modified by the conquering Spaniards of the 1500s and, later, by the rest of the world, well into the twentieth century. In an ironic turn of history, modern nutritionists have come full circle in their quest to unlock the complexity of the rich, decadent treat we know today as chocolate: they have "discovered" the chemical compounds in dark chocolate that provide its nutritional and therapeutic value, scientific verification of an intuitive wisdom several millennia old.

pre-columbian prescriptions

Within a pre-Columbian worldview, supernatural forces were responsible for the maladies and diseases of everyday life. For example, the Maya Underworld of Xibalba was a "place of fright" that evoked horrific images of disease, fever, and filth. Ruled by One Death and Seven Death, it was home to lords with such names as "Scab Stripper, Blood Gatherer, Demon of Pus, Demon of Jaundice, Bone Scepter and Skull Scepter, Demon of Filth and Demon of Woe" (fig. 5.1). Their sole mandate was to manifest disease and affliction on humankind: "to draw blood from people . . . to make people swell up . . . to make pus come out of their legs . . . to make their faces yellow . . . to

Figure 5.1   Underworld gods and creatures. Left to right: Toad, the rain god Chac, the creator god as a baby, Waterlily Jaguar, Firefly. (Late Classic Maya cylindrical vessel)

reduce people to bones."[1] Not even today's most spine-chilling horror film could match this drama of pestilence-filled terror!

The application of medicinal cacao to remedy such afflictions is documented in the books of Chilam Balam and *The Ritual of the Bacabs*, eighteenth-century Yucatan manuscripts that are copies of more ancient codices. Reflecting the language and cadence of a much earlier era, *The Ritual of the Bacabs* draws us into a world of ancient practices where priests and shamans used their powers to deliver individuals from disease and affliction. It is filled with nearly fifty incantations of curing and healing chanted by Maya healers during rites to cure skin eruptions, fevers, and seizures. They called on the gods for assistance and administered herbal concoctions to the sick, whose illnesses were often blamed on personified spirits. The healers skillfully coaxed diseases out of the body by appealing to the invading spirit's appreciation of not only poetry and logic but also to the spirit's goodwill. Many of these botanical remedies contained cacao as part of the recipe; an example is *chacah*, or medicinal chocolate, a drink of cacao blended with honey, pepper, and tobacco juice, administered to a patient at the end of one such chant.[2]

The medicinal cures with cacao prescribed in the *Book of Chilam Balam of Nah* reflect a similar mind-set. Dysentery was cured with five cacao beans and the bark of several plants, including avocado. A more lively concoction was recommended for the

Figure 5.2   An example of illustrations accompanying accounts of diseased and sick individuals in Aztec codices. (Codex Borgia)

retention of urine: a warm drink of ground cacao, cochineal (insects used for red dye), and a cricket.[3]

But the early colonial writings of the sixteenth century that documented the life, plants, and medicines of Aztecs and other Mexica peoples provide an even more definitive understanding of the medicinal use of cacao. Accounts of epidemics and disease, with depictions of vomiting and diarrhea, appear throughout many codices (fig. 5.2). The Aztecs' superior knowledge of plant chemistry and pharmaceuticals impressed the Spaniards arriving in the New World. Their medical doctrine had not changed

Figure 5.3   A sixteenth-century woodcut of an astrological chart showing the four temperaments (phlegmatic, sanguine, melancholic, and choleric) caused by the humoral fluids phlegm, blood, black bile, and yellow bile, respectively. (Sixteenth-century engraving from Quinta Essentia, *by Leonhart Thurneisser zum Thurn)*

much since the time of Hippocrates and was based on the premise that good health depended on a balance between the zodiac and the body's "humors" and the related temperaments, called phlegmatic, sanguine, choleric, and melancholic (fig. 5.3). Under this European system, four different types of humors resided in the human body: blood (hot and moist), phlegm (cold and moist), yellow bile (hot and dry), and black bile (cold and dry). The Aztecs defined illnesses using a similar structure of paired opposites: hot/cold, dark/light, humidity/drought, weakness/strength. Within a Mesoamerican worldview, gods dominated all medical and dietary conditions, while various evil winds, inanimate objects, and animal spirits actually inhabited the body and caused disease (fig. 5.4).[4]

But healing practices were not completely dominated by this religious mind-set. The Aztecs in particular had long been cultivating plants for medicinal purposes in

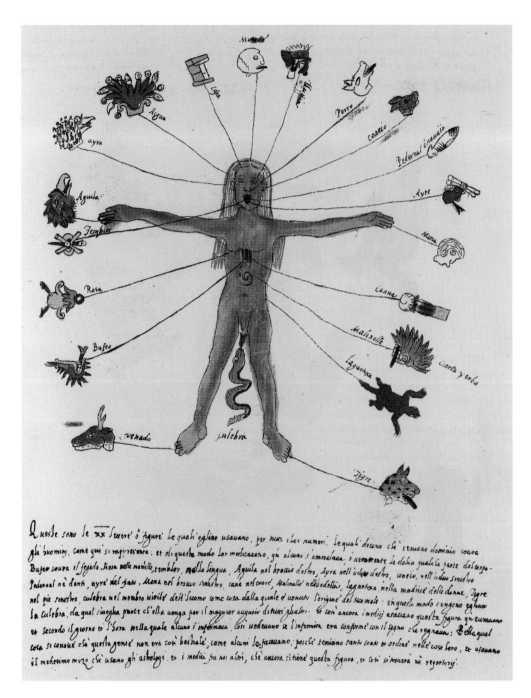

Figure 5.4   An Aztec diagram of animal spirits that cause disease in the body. (Rios Codex)

Figure 5.5   The garden of Huaxtepec, Mexico, where cacao trees and other botanical species were grown, depicted in a sixteenth-century map from the "Relación Geografica de Guaxtepec" (JGI XXIV-3).

botanical gardens. One of the more ambitious botanical ventures in the New World was the garden at Huaxtepec (Oaxtepec in modern-day Morelos). Prior to his death in 1469, Tenochtitlan's King Moctezuma I had ordered that cacao trees and other plants, many of which were used in the cacao drink, be transplanted from the "Hot Country near the coast" to the springs of Huaxtepec (fig. 5.5). The plants were transported wrapped in cloth with dirt around their roots. This highly successful transplanting, while giving Aztecs "the refreshment and delights" of cacao and other plants and flowers, created a marvelous testing laboratory for medicinal plants.[5]

European intrigue with Mesoamerican remedies prompted shipments of rainforest plants across the ocean to Spain for medicinal applications. This vast pharmacopoeia of strange new flora from the New World motivated Francisco Hernández, the royal physician to Spain's King Phillip II, to investigate firsthand and report back to the Crown.[6] In his extensive study of Mexican and Central American plants, published as *Historia de las Plantas de la Nueva España* in 1577, Hernández followed the dogma of the time, classifying all Mesoamerican plants as hot, cold, wet, or dry.

The first "scientific" description of cacao came from this early study. Chocolate was "temperate in nature, but leaning to the cold and humid . . . on the whole it is very nourishing. Because of its cool nature, drinks made from it are good in hot weather, and to cure fevers." If mixed with other additives, the chocolate drink "could excite the venereal appetite."[7] Even though Hernández may have realized that chocolate taken alone did not create an aphrodisiacal effect, its reputation as a love potion has, for centuries, been the subject of intense consideration on both sides of the Atlantic.

chocolate as a cure-all

During this period of excitement about New World plants, chocolate entered the European mind-set as a curative. The Spaniards observed the Aztecs not only drinking chocolate as a sacred and pleasurable beverage but also using it to alleviate a range of mental and physical ailments. Chocolate, it seemed, had the power to improve the probability of conception and the quality of breast milk or reverse the effects of exhaustion, impotence, vision-quest hangovers, mental illness, fevers, poison, skin eruptions, lung problems, agitation, diarrhea, indigestion, and flatulence, to name a few.[8] In an improbable speculation, some thought that drinking chocolate in the morning could provide immunity to a poisonous snake's bite in the afternoon, a folk-medicine warning recorded by Oviedo y Valdés during his travels among native Nicaraguans in the mid-sixteenth century.[9]

The Florentine Codex, written by Sahagún in the late sixteenth century, best describes medicinal cacao when ground up with other ingredients (many from the same rainforest environment) that had curative properties. Combined with the bark of the rubber tree (*Castilla elastica*), cacao was used to treat infections; when mixed with the root of *tlayapoloni xiuitl* (genus and species unknown), it was taken as a remedy for childhood diarrhea. Fever and faintness required a different concoction of ground cacao, maize, and *tlacoxochitl* (*Bouvardia termifolia*, the cigar plant).[10] Cacao combined with dried *cacahauxochitl* (flor de cacao, *Quararibea funebris*), whose fragrance can

Figure 5.6 Sixteenth-century illustration of flor de cacao, or cacahuaxochitl, from De historia general de las cosas de Nueva España (Florentine Codex).

linger for decades, reduced anxiety, fever, and coughs (fig. 5.6). Alkaloids found in *Quararibea funebris* most likely give it its medicinal attributes.

An odd drink of ground cacao and ground *quinametli* (called the "bones of ancient people" by Sahagún), mixed with softened maize tamales, was a remedy for one who "passes blood." And best of all, phlegmatic coughs were cured with a two-step remedy of opossum tail followed by chocolate mixed with three other tasty additives as a chaser.[11] Probably cacao was not the active agent in this formula and other concoctions. Instead, it may have been used as a medium to administer drugs or was added to various mixtures to disguise the repugnant taste of more-noxious ingredients.

Other components of the cacao tree—bark, butter, leaves, flowers—were used by the Aztecs in cosmetics applications and to treat burns, cuts, and various skin irritations. The modern-day inclusion of cacao fat in suppositories may have started

with the Maya, who administered hallucinogenic enemas during vision-quest rituals, aided, perhaps, by cacao fat as a natural lubricant. Alternatively, liquid cacao may have been used as one of the ingredients in a hallucinogenic enema mix.[12] Indeed, numerous Maya vases depict scenes of enemas being given in social settings (fig. 5.7).

At first, the Spanish invaders avoided chocolate, despite their desire for remedies to ease ailments contracted in the field or brought from Europe—gout, diarrhea, wound infections, asthma, indigestion, scurvy, syphilis, fatigue. During Cortés's march from Veracruz to Tenochtitlan in 1521, the soldier Bernal Diaz del Castillo was one of the first to document his fellow Europeans' reaction to chocolate: "When it came time to drink the chocolate that had been brought them, that most highly prized drink of the Indian, they were filled with fear. When the Indians saw that they dared not drink they tasted from all the gourds and the Spanish then quenched their thirst with chocolate and realized what a refreshing drink it was."[13] The sixteenth-century Italian Girolamo Benzoni came to the same conclusion after initially thinking it "more a drink for pigs than a drink for humanity." After refusing for a full year to taste it, he finally was won over by its satiating superiority over wine.[14]

Figure 5.7   A domestic scene of enemas being given; the pots of enema brew may contain cacao fat as a lubricant or ingredient. (Late Classic Maya cylindrical vessel)

chocolate as a stimulant

One of the first things the adventurers realized about chocolate was that it boosted energy, a fact well understood by Mesoamericans. Puzzled Europeans had not yet embraced the stimulating effects of coffee or tea, although they were quite familiar with alcohol and had tried unsuccessfully to adjust to New World intoxicants such as fermented maize drinks and *pulque,* a stupor-producing concoction made from the agave plant. The effect of chocolate was a very different experience: it kept them awake. To their amazement, the Spaniards noticed that Aztec soldiers were able to march for a whole day with nothing to eat but chocolate, which was especially effective during times of physical hardship. (The Hershey Chocolate Company capitalized on this fact centuries later by including a chocolate bar in food-ration boxes for soldiers in both world wars.)

Chocolate's significance as an energizer may be reflected in artwork of the Classic period Maya. The exquisite clay figurine shown in figure 5.8 from Jaina Island off Campeche, Mexico, expresses an age-old belief that one is invincible, energized, perhaps made stronger if protected by cacao. In this example, multiridged cacao pods sprout from the armor of an esteemed warrior who is dressed and ready for battle with cacao icons, as talismans, to carry him forward.

Chocolate's idealized role as ritual food for gods, kings, and warriors, as well as helpmate of the soul, may stem from its chemical composition. Pure dark chocolate releases endorphins that jolt the brain with a short-lived euphoric uplift. It contains several potent compounds. Two of them, theobromine and caffeine, keep us alert. As a bitter, volatile alkaloid, theobromine resembles caffeine in chemical structure. Although there is ten times more theobromine than caffeine in dark chocolate, some scientists believe that the stimulating effect of theobromine, significantly weaker than that of caffeine, may be too low to achieve such mind-altering effects as caffeine produces.[15] Although the verdict is still out on these psychopharmacological effects, our experience with pure, unadulterated chocolate, fresh off the metate, is that it kept us up all night!

Figure 5.8   A warrior in cacao armor. (Late Classic Maya clay figurine from Campeche, Mexico)

chocolate: a peal struck with the pevil?

Because of the limited amount of scientific knowledge available in the sixteenth century, magic and superstition played a prominent role in explaining chocolate's psychoactive properties for Europeans and Mesoamericans alike. Initial European accounts described chocolate as mysterious or even relegated this substance to the work of the devil. This was a typical European response to many poorly understood New World substances and behaviors, so it is no surprise that chocolate, a stimulant that made one feel good, fell into this ill-defined rubric. Concurrent with the time period surrounding the sixteenth century, religious zealots of the Church and Crown maintained their unified world supremacy by exterminating nonbelievers (Jews, Protestants, Muslims). During this Spanish Inquisition, the euphoria brought on by non-Catholic foods and customs was highly suspicious. In fact, merely eating the wrong ethnic food in Spain could result in one's torture and death. Even as some critics warned against falling under the devil's influence or stated that chocolate created "thick and sticky humors" and exacerbated melancholic or phlegmatic conditions, the newcomers quickly became enthralled with chocolate's positive attributes.[16]

chocolate and romance

One of these attributes included the alluring promise that chocolate might be employed as an aphrodisiac. Events surrounding the polygamous Aztec ruler Moctezuma led to early misconceptions about chocolate's role in matters of lovemaking. Bernal Diaz del Castillo observed that women served their ruler fifty golden cups of chocolate at a palace feast at Tenochtitlan. He further concluded that the chocolate was for Moctezuma's success with women, an observation that forever sealed chocolate's reputation as an aphrodisiac among lustful Europeans.[17]

Down through the ages, chocolate has been offered as a love token, but little evidence has thus far come to light that chocolate acts as a natural aphrodisiac, except by keeping one alert. The Badianus Manuscript, also known as *Libellus de Medicinalibus Indorum Herbis*, a sixteenth-century herbal directory of Mesoamerican plants written by Aztec physician Martin de la Cruz, suggested that crushed heart flower (*Talauma mexicana*), called *yolloxochitl* by the Aztecs and *flor de corazón* by the Spanish, could be taken to cure "sterility" (fig. 5.9). Although the word *sterility* is not defined and may refer to female issues, male impotence may be synonymous in this case. Curiously, one of Moctezuma's favorite cacao beverages was made of ground cacao mixed with heart flower, which tastes a bit like sweet melon. Traditionally, the flowers, leaves,

and bark of *Talauma mexicana* have been used to treat "fright sickness," melancholy, heartache, and a host of other ills that plague the stomach, breast, and heart.

The very fragrant heart flower was a favored additive to cacao drinks and was known to produce a digitalis-like effect; it is still used for this purpose by cardiac patients in areas of rural Mexico. Chocolate's early pairing with heart flower may have placed chocolate in the same medicinal category as a vasodilator for the heart and other organs. Modern pharmacological studies of the heart flower have isolated the glucosides, alkaloids, terpenes, and steroids that may be responsible for its effect on cardiac function and blood pressure.[18]

Vanilla (*Vanilla planifolia*), another rumored aphrodisiac paired with chocolate, is an orchid indigenous to the tropical forests of Mexico. Known to the Aztecs as *tlilxochitl*, the climbing vine grew in the same lowland shade environments as the esteemed cacao tree and perhaps even used the cacao tree as support (fig. 5.10). When properly cured, fermented, and dried, the tiny black seeds (thousands of which can be

Figure 5.9 (left)   A sixteenth-century illustration of heart flower, yoloxochitl, from the Badianus Manuscript, *an Aztec herbal of 1552.*

Figure 5.10 (right)   A sixteenth-century illustration of vanilla, tlilxochitl, from the Badianus Manuscript, *an Aztec herbal of 1552.*

extracted from each eight- to ten-inch-long stringy pod) produce a heavenly fragrance. From ancient times to the present, this powerful aromatic stimulant has been credited with promoting sexual desires while exhilarating the brain.

Besides the addition of flowers and spices to cacao to enhance desire, the cacao bean itself has been used as a symbol for female genitalia (the longitudinal crease on the bean resembles a vulva), a representation that has continued into the twentieth century. During a Yucatec Maya curing ceremony performed in the 1990s, Betty Faust observed a rite involving an adolescent girl with psychological problems. The girl was initiated into womanhood with the help of a healer-priest who employed traditional objects and medicinal plants during the lengthy incantation. Five candles placed on the altar represented the four cardinal directions, while the one in the middle held up the universe, forming the quincunx of Maya cosmology. During the ceremony, two pairs of cacao beans were arranged with two pairs of chili peppers on either side of the candles. These represented the biological union of male and female in an ordered universe with the cacao beans symbolizing female genitalia, and chili peppers the male penis. The number of cacao beans and chili peppers totaled twenty each, or two human beings (the ancient Maya associated a complete human being with the number twenty). Later, the cacao beans and chili peppers were buried along with other ritual food items in a pit, a symbolic meal offering to the Lords of the Underworld and a substitute for the patient herself.[19]

chocolate: A vehicle for poison and Hallucinogens

Observers of New World behavior noted that chocolate was sometimes paired with psychoactive substances during vision-quest rituals. In addition, Sahagún observed that "green" or raw cacao may have contributed to drunkenness and disorientation, and there is evidence in Maya iconography that cacao was drunk as an alcoholic beverage. The alcohol was most likely produced from the sugar of the remaining pulp surrounding the beans during the fermentation process. On Lintel 3 from Piedras Negras, Guatemala (fig. 5.11), the glyphic text reveals that an alcoholic drink of fermented cacao was served at a three-day feast of ritual dance and drunkenness honoring Ruler 4, Hoy Uk Kían. The fermented cacao was probably in the tripod cylinder vessel on the ground that divides the two seated groups of festive participants.[20] In modern-day Tabasco, one can still buy cacao wine on the roadside.

But in most instances, chocolate was paired with hallucinogenic agents to disguise a bitter taste or was employed as a chaser after ingesting psilocybin mushrooms

(*Psilocybin cubensis*) or smoking jimsonweed (*Datura stramonium*). Oviedo y Valdés observed a ritual in 1528 among a gathering of Nicaraguans during which gourds of cacao were passed from hand to hand between puffs of smoke inhaled from a ceremonial pipe. After much drumming and singing, the men fell senseless on the ground or ran amok weeping and howling and had to be carried off to bed by their wives or friends.[21] Chocolate was later administered to cure "stupidity of mind" during their days of recovery.

As much as hippies from the 1960s would like to take credit for marijuana brownies à la Alice B. Toklas, the culinary technique of combining chocolate with drugs for that extra buzz has been around for centuries. Modern studies show that the effects of marijuana may be heightened if it is mixed with chocolate. Chocolate contains three unsaturated N-acylethanolamines that could act as cannabinoid mimics either directly by activating cannabinoid receptors in the brain or indirectly by increasing anandamide lipid levels, which heightens the euphoric experience.[22]

Chocolate was also handily employed as a vehicle to poison one's enemies. One

Figure 5.11   The glyphic text in the second row of the upper band reveals that an alcoholic drink of fermented cacao in a tripod vase (lower center) was drunk during a three-day ritual honoring a ruler. (Late Classic Maya, carved stone Lintel 3, Piedras Negras, Guatemala)

account stands out as particularly excessive. The colonial women of Chiapas, Mexico, used chocolate to poison their priest after he had forbidden them to drink chocolate during church services, threatening excommunication if they continued. Rather than heeding his demands, the women opted to get rid of their long-winded priest. They administered their poetic justice by serving poison with his daily cup of hot chocolate, giving a different meaning to our current "death by chocolate" mantra. This delicious tale has a dark motive, and the version has undoubtedly been embellished over time, but accounts through the ages indicate that chocolate was effectively used to mask the taste of lethal poisons. In Mesoamerica, given the easy access to both cacao and poisonous plants, one had to be on the lookout for such duplicitous behavior.

Chocolate can be lethal on its own, however, for dogs. The theobromine in chocolate overstimulates the dog's heart muscle, causing epileptic seizures and death. Were the ancient Maya aware of this canine reaction to chocolate? They did offer a dog with spots the color of cacao to various deities during cacao harvesting festivals. Whether or not they fed him chocolate beforehand, we will never know.

chocolate: Body and Heart

Pharmacological studies of recent years indicate that the ancient Mesoamericans were not far off in holding cacao in such high esteem. Dark chocolate is a very rich source of minerals and trace elements, exceeding almost every other food. We humans require no less than fourteen of these minerals for our bodies to function properly. Chocolate is a veritable storehouse of these elements, especially copper and magnesium.[23]

Unfortunately, the excessive use of sweetening products along with vegetable fat and powder in today's commercial chocolate has led some to consider chocolate a fattening, tooth-rotting, addictive indulgence that causes poor health. Fresh cacao beans, however, contain only 2–4 percent free sugars and traces of sugar alcohols. In well-fermented beans, the sucrose can be dramatically decreased until it is near zero as fructose and glucose are increased.[24]

One of the most confusing aspects about the cacao butter found in chocolate is its high level of saturated fat, which is known to clog arteries and increase cholesterol levels—two risk indicators for heart attacks. But not all saturated fats are the same. The saturated fat in cacao butter contains high amounts of stearic and oleic acids that counteract these negative effects by reducing fat absorption dramatically; much of the cacao butter we eat simply passes through our body.[25]

But the most exciting revelation about dark chocolate is its high flavonoid content and substantial antioxidant capacity. This composition gives chocolate the ability to fight free radicals that cause degenerative diseases in humans. The flavonoids are four to five times stronger than those of black tea, two to three times stronger than green tea, and almost two times stronger than red wine.[26] A healthful consumption of flavonol-rich chocolate may prevent stroke, coronary disease, and possibly dementia, by dilating the blood vessels in humans!

One modern culture may be living proof of the longevity-inducing benefits of dark chocolate. The indigenous Kunas, who live in the isolated San Blas island chain off the coast of Panama, drink dark chocolate as part of their daily routine (at almost every meal). Yet one study concluded that they have no increase in blood pressure and hypertension as they age despite their high salt intake. Conversely, the Kunas who have migrated to Panama City and do not drink dark chocolate, or drink adulterated versions of the drink, fared as poorly as urban Caucasians in the study in having high blood pressure.[27]

The Maya and others may have arrived at similar conclusions, observing, perhaps, that those who drank chocolate lived longer; this may be one reason that the drink was restricted to royalty, who had claims on immortality. When Sahagún made the analogy that the cacao pod was like the human heart, in that they both contained something precious—blood, and liquid chocolate—he certainly was not aware that chocolate actually protected the heart. But then again, if chocolate could sustain the journeying soul after death, why could it not do the same for the beating heart in life?

Balancing the cosmos: chocolate's Role in Rainforest Ecology

6

Here's this ecosystem built around a treat that could be good for the world.

John Lunde, director, International Environmental Programs, M&M/Mars

The tropical forest system where undomesticated cacao thrives is a biologically diverse and interdependent universe of plants, animals, insects, and nutrients. Here, all things are essential for regeneration. Ecological order was at the heart of a pre-Columbian cosmic view in which human destiny depended on the predictability of the natural seasons and the celestial movements of the sun, moon, and stars. If climate changes, drought, or famine disrupted the normal state of equilibrium, Mesoamericans turned to offerings, sacrifice, and prophecy in hopes of its restoration.

A Cha'-Chak ceremony to ensure rain may be taking place in the vase scene in figure 6.1, showing the Aztec rain god, Tlaloc, grasping cacao tree limbs as he performs a ritual. Images such as this from pre-Columbian art remind us that the cacao tree is not only linked to human and cosmic regeneration but also is essential to biological order within the natural world. The interconnections between the cacao tree and other rainforest flora and fauna take on even more poignancy today as dwindling tropical environments, disappearing species, and global warming strain our earth's vitality.

Figure 6.1 The Aztec rain god, Tlaloc, grasping cacao tree limbs. (Early Classic tripod vase found at Tikal)

Trees and Forests: Ancient Order

The mythological worlds of Mesoamerica provide some of the first clues to cacao's function within a greater ecological realm. In several creation stories, forest trees were essential for the cosmic balance that was achieved after several cycles of destruction. In some of these stories, five color-coded trees delineated the four corners and the central point, or axis mundi, of the universe. The books of Chilam Balam of Chumayel and Tizimin called each of these First Trees an *imix-ché* (*imix*, "first"; *ché/té*, "tree"). Although this term can take on multidimensional meanings, the writers of the Chumayel and Tizimin may have possibly made a double play on words, alluding to a "Crocodile Tree." Imix is the Maya equivalent of the Mexican Cipactli, the supernatural crocodile. (The first day of the Maya calendar is Imix, and the first day of the Aztec calendar is Cipactli.)

In Maya cosmology, this fantastic crocodile not only floats in a primordial sea as the horizontal surface of the earth but also, according to some scholars, is raised up vertically as a World Tree in the sky as the Milky Way.[1] Some of the earliest known Crocodile Tree imagery, with the crocodile's mouth and feet at the "roots" and its tail alluding to "branches" of a metaphorical tree, comes from Preclassic Izapa, Chiapas, located within the cacao-rich Soconusco region. The natural world may explain such imagery: crocodiles lay their eggs within mounds of earth they pile up along the water, and tree saplings root in these mounds, creating a diminutive version of the earth's surface.[2]

The cacao tree was sometimes depicted as a Crocodile Tree, as a Classic period incensario or censer (*saklaktun*) from Copan, Honduras, suggests (fig. 6.2). The scales on the snout at the base of this inverted crocodile are transformed into cacao pods as they progress up the lid and appear prominently from its tail "branches."[3] This allusion is repeated on a stone fragment from Chichen Itza (fig. 6.3), on which an inverted Crocodile Tree laden with cacao pods is carved.[4] Both of these visual metaphors suggest that the cacao tree may have been viewed in some Mesoamerican areas as a significant imix ché, a tree pivotal to environmental stability since the beginning of time.

In the Chumayel, the imix-ché trees that established the limits of the cosmos also provided the sustainable environment for the sacred chocolate tree. The five directional trees were set up as records of "the destruction of the world," much in the same way, perhaps, that reforestation can occur after major environmental degradation. Not until these trees were "raised" could all the life forms on earth spring forth, including the "five leafed flower, the five drooping [petals], the cacao [with grains like] a row of teeth."[5] It was as if one great forest finally sustained stability and a fine-tuned ecosystem.

Chapter Six

An Early Classic period vase (fig. 6.4) from Guatemala depicts such a natural environment. A stylized cacao tree on its lid grows from a tropical forest environment of various animals, monkeys, plants, and birds incised on the vase and lid. The creator god, Itzamna, barely visible on the back panel (not in view), seems to have finally emerged, perhaps from the Underworld, on the visible front panel. The glyphs on this vessel indicate that it was intended for cacao; a glyph on top of the cacao tree tells us that we are in a celestial realm. Four cacao pods—positioned to indicate the four cardinal directions—suggest that this cacao tree is a World Tree; eight additional cacao pods on the lid possibly represent intercardinal directions. Nine pods are also attached to the vase around the bottom. In combination, the various flora, fauna,

Figure 6.2 (left) A stylized cacao tree depicted as the Crocodile Tree. (Late Classic Maya stone censer from Copan, Honduras)

Figure 6.3 (right) A stylized cacao tree depicted as the Crocodile Tree. (Late Classic Maya stone relief from Chichen Itza)

Figure 6.4 An incised vessel depicts a biologically diverse, tropical forest environment. A stylized cacao tree emerging from the lid bears a celestial glyph at its top. Cacao pods on the tree and on the lid indicate cardinal and intercardinal directions. Monkeys, birds, and vegetation appear on the vessel and lid while Itzamna, the creator god, emerges from the Underworld. Glyphic text on side panels (not visible) reveals that the vessel was for "fresh" cacao. (Early Classic tripod vase, Guatemala)

and celestial elements depicted here perhaps symbolize a belief that the cacao tree, plants, animals, and the entire multilayered structure of the forests and cosmos were interdependent.

Such a symbiotic universe, delineated by cosmic trees that bound the perimeters of human space, emerged later as a concept with the adoption of agriculture as a way of life, when the four-sided agricultural plot became an essential component of settled village life and human subsistence. Delineation of agricultural fields by guardian trees, endowed with special powers, protected agricultural lands from wild animals and evil forest-dwelling spirits. In contrast to these sunlit artificial spaces, forests were considered dangerous places of shaded darkness, a haven for venomous snakes, jaguars, poisonous plants, and demons. However ominous, the ancient forests were essential to survival as a source of sustenance for humans and animals and were seen as a place where supernatural powers resided.[6]

cacao and biodiversity: protection, nutrients, and propagation

The cacao tree promotes biodiversity because it requires a fine-tuned ecosystem to survive: it is wind sensitive, sun sensitive, drought sensitive, and nitrogen dependent. Cacao trees thrive in the humid, high-rainfall environments located within twenty degrees north and south of the equator; they cannot exist in climates that have minimum temperatures below 32°F or have dry seasons longer than four months.[7] A layered canopy of taller trees protects the shade-loving cacao tree and its delicate roots from direct sunlight, wind, and driving rains. In its natural habitat of a densely shaded rainforest, the wild cacao tree is lanky, reaching a height of fifty feet, and grows tightly spaced in clumps. In cultivated situations, where tree thinning allows more filtered light, it is fuller and shorter. Large leaves, which alternate in two rows on the branches, range in color from pinkish green to silvery green to deep green. The tree's long, shallow roots, with hairlike tentacles, are nurtured by rotting pods, plant debris, leaf litter, and organic mulch layered on the rainforest floor (fig. 6.5).

Several tree species have been recognized as "protectors" of the cacao tree, including the tree of inferior cacao, *Theobroma bicolor*, or pataxte (*balam-té*: "protector tree," "jaguar tree") and the coral tree (*Erythrina corallodendron*), the "talking tree" (fig. 6.6). One tropical tree in particular, however, the canté tree (*Gliricidia sepium*), commonly called *madre de cacao* in Spanish, has been well recognized since ancient times. It not only protects the cacao tree from sun, wind, and driving rains but also provides a constant source of nitrogen-fixing bacteria to the cacao's shallow root system through its

Figure 6.5 *A cacao tree in a forest setting near Tabasco, Mexico, showing the canopy and leaf litter.*

root nodules and leaf matter. This natural symbiotic relationship is further strengthened by the small amounts of coumarin its leaf matter leeches into the soil, thus releasing a natural pesticide to rodents that covet the cacao pod for its sweet pulp.[8] The canté tree appears in the epic Popol Vuh myth as the Yellow Tree, so named because of the yellow dye extracted from it.[9] It was also an imix ché in the Book of Chilam Balam of Chumayel, the yellow World Tree to the south at the time of creation.[10]

The cacao tree's botanical structure is essential to its pollination. Its small white, or pink, starlike flowers grow directly along the tree's trunk and the larger branches (fig. 6.7), an adaptation called cauliflory that evolved to facilitate pollination by insects, ants, and other small animals that crawl on the trunk.

While numerous tiny creatures are attracted to the rotting, sugary pulp that oozes from broken cacao pods on the ground, a certain variety of midge fly species (the Ceratopogonidae of the dipteran family) serves as the primary pollinator of the cacao tree

Figure 6.7   Cacao flowers on the trunk of a tree.

Figure 6.6   "Talking Tree." (Late Classic Maya cylindrical vase)

flower. Midges, which beat their wings at a thousand times per second—faster than any other animal on the planet—frequently lay their eggs in rotten, rain-filled cacao husks. Cacao trees do not do well naturally in environments lacking midges, and shaded forests with a plethora of vines, bromeliads, mistletoe, and orchids, where midges frequently breed, usually host a greater variety and number of midge species.

Most of the pollinating midges are female, and their timing is important. Each cacao flower opens only once, beginning at late afternoon and continuing through the

Figure 6.8   A monkey holding a split cacao pod. (Late Classic Maya cylindrical vase)

night, and the flowers are most receptive to pollination at dawn. If pollination does not occur within forty-eight hours, the flowers fall off the tree, creating a blanket of white petals on the forest floor. Only 1 to 5 percent of the cacao tree's flowers produce cacao pods. Other cacao flower visitors include the stingless bee, *Trigona jaty*, which is referred to as a "pollen thief," one that steals pollen or nectar without pollinating the flower. Surprisingly, honeybees are not at all attracted to the cacao flower.[11] So those biting midges, pesky no-see-ums that can drive one crazy at sunup and sundown, at least do their part by bringing us chocolate.

Animals that are similarly attracted to the sweet and nutritious pulp—spider and howler monkeys, bats, birds, squirrels (see figure on dedication page), and other rodents—become unwitting propagators of cacao by dispersing seeds or by damaging the pods enough so that pollinators can lay eggs in them. These animals gnaw at the pods or peck holes (in the case of woodpeckers and other birds) in them to get at

the nutritious, sweet inner layer where the seeds are embedded. Monkeys, being especially cunning at breaking open cacao pods, are probably the most successful propagators (fig. 6.8). They extract the pulp and carry it off like a bunch of precious grapes to another area in the forest where they suck on the pulp, inadvertently releasing the bitter seeds (fig. 6.9).[12] The sweetness of the pulp is the key to the tree's reproductive strategy, because once the animal chews open the pod, the otherwise imprisoned seeds can spill out. Unlike most fruits, ripe cacao pods rarely fall naturally from the tree; they need help from animals, and humans too.[13]

Several endangered species depend for their own survival on the same biodiverse, shaded-forest habitat that nurtures the cacao tree. One that immediately comes

Figure 6.9   A monkey running off with cacao pulp. (Late Classic Maya cylindrical vase)

Figure 6.10   The endangered pink-legged graveteiro and golden-headed lion tamarin, as found in Brazil's rustic cacao plantations.

to mind is the jaguar, the majestic feline that has woven in and out of cacao groves for thousands of years and was paired with cacao artistically throughout Maya prehistory. Another, discovered by ornithologists, is a new type of ovenbird species, the pink-legged graveteiro, which nests exclusively in the canopy of Brazil's shaded cacao plantations. Also, the rare and timid golden-headed lion tamarin (fig. 6.10) makes its home in cacao orchards that have a variety of plant species.[14] Because monkeys and other arboreal primates require such an environment for feeding and social activities, ecologists are now using their presence to assess the health of Latin America's rainforests and agroforestry systems.[15]

Figure 6.11   A ceramic cacao pod, probably of the criollo variety, from the vicinity of Chichicastenango, Guatemala.

Human Manipulation of cacao Environments: Ancient Groves

DNA studies have pinpointed two areas that gave rise to two slightly different cacao genotypes, which have cross-pollinated, both naturally and by cultivators, to create all of the known varieties that one sees today. In the lower Amazon, a type of *Theobroma cacao* known as *forastero* (*T. cacao* subsp. *sphaerocarpum*) grew wild along the alluvial basin. In pre-Hispanic times, the delicious pulp of this smooth-skinned, melon-shaped cacao was originally eaten only as a fruit. The second area, closer to the Caribbean in the foothills of the Venezuelan and Colombian Andes, was home to another type, *criollo* (*T. cacao* subsp. *cacao*). This flavorful Venezuelan cacao, named *criollo* by the Spanish, produced small, warty, multiridged pods with pointy tips and was probably the ancestor to all the varieties of cultivated cacao in pre-Hispanic Central America and Mexico (fig. 6.11).[16]

Although researchers know that humans have manipulated cacao's natural environment throughout several millennia, they have not pinpointed when the cultivation of cacao actually began. Cacao cultivation existed within a variety of habitats, from kitchen gardens and ancestral orchards to large-scale microenvironments of natural sinkholes. The ancient Maya may have initially cultivated cacao in small, scattered clumps similar to how cacao grew in the wild.[17] Before being deliberately cultivated by humans, groves of wild cacao probably flourished along alluvial river valleys, shaded ecosystems readily adaptable to horticultural practices by people living along the eastern river systems of the Caribbean watershed.[18] On the Pacific slope and piedmont in what is now Guatemala, El Salvador, and Nicaragua—areas with distinctive alternating wet and dry seasons—cleverly engineered ditch-irrigation systems enabled the cultivation of cacao trees. Such irrigation systems were in existence at the time of the conquest, when the Pipil-Nicarao peoples inhabited this region.[19] But recent archaeological evidence in Guatemala's Suchitepequez/Boca Costa region around Chocolá seems to support the view that irrigation systems were in place as early as 200 BC.[20]

By the time of the Spanish arrival, the area below Lake Atitlan, Guatemala, was one of the most prolific ancient centers of cacao production, as exhibited by place-names such as Chicacao ("By the Cacao Groves"), PanNan ("Place of Our Mother, Cacao"), and Suchitepequez or Kotz'eej ("Flowering Mountain") in Tz'utujile Maya. The latter was probably named for the abundant sea of flowers covering the zapote and cacao trees that once thrived there, a region where indigenous populations owned and cultivated large cacao orchards and plantations.[21]

Pedro de Alvarado's second letter to Hernán Cortés gives us some idea of how extensive the forests and the cacao orchards were in the Suchitepequez/Boca Costa region of Guatemala. He describes how he and his men had to force their way through dense forests and cacao orchards on their way to Zapotitlan.[22] And in the Soconusco region of Chiapas, as many as 1,600,000 cacao trees were possibly under cultivation by the late sixteenth century.[23] What happened to them?

Myriad factors contributed to the diminished presence of cacao. Postcontact deforestation and the massive deaths of skilled indigenous labor during the sixteenth- and seventeenth-century epidemics shifted the cacao industry to other regions within the Spanish-controlled realm. By the early part of the nineteenth century, cacao orchards had become smaller and smaller. Historic records from the Soconusco region suggest that disease, pests, and natural disasters such as droughts and hurricanes destroyed cacao groves; with larger plantations more vulnerable to these unpredictable forces, downsizing may have been a logical response. However, the reduced size of plantations, coupled with the rise of cattle ranching and the late-nineteenth-century introduction of coffee cultivation in the region, took more and more precious land away from the sacred cacao tree.[24]

Today, the birthplace of cacao cultivation, Mexico and Central America, produces only small amounts of cacao for the international market. While the world's market relies on large-scale commercial plantations established in Brazil, Venezuela, the

Ivory Coast of Africa, and Indonesia, most of the chocolate grown in southern Mexico and Central America is for local consumption, with Tabasco supplying 80 percent of that local market.

Ancient and current Deforestation

The topographical shift in Mexico and Central America from ancient forests to huge tracts of agricultural lands with relatively little surrounding forest has inverted the ecological balance between human and natural spaces. Deforestation itself is nothing new for Mesoamerica, however. Long before the Classic-period construction of large Maya cities, the abandonment of earlier settlements occurred, probably as a result of periods of drought, famine, and degradation of outlying wetlands, agricultural lands, and forests. In fact, pollen records reveal that forest disturbance and plant manipulation started as long ago as 10,000 BC and intensified by 2000–1000 BC in the Maya lowlands.[25]

For example, the demise of El Mirador, a grand Preclassic metropolis located in Guatemala's Peten rainforest, may have been caused by degradation of soils from intensive agriculture near the settlement. Ironically, the site's future is now the subject of intense conflict between modern-day archaeologists who want to save the area as an archaeological preserve and local villagers who fight for the right to log their forest to clear land for cattle ranching.[26] Clear-cutting has impacted the primeval forests of the Maya lowlands for a thousand years; trees were chopped primarily for agriculture, cooking, fuel, and lime making to plaster the surfaces of large-scale construction projects (which required massive amounts of fuel to burn the limestone).[27]

Volcanic activity, followed within a few years by drought, famine, and disease, may have been one of several factors contributing to the Classic Maya collapse and may have caused earlier hiatus intervals in Mesoamerica's prehistory. Agrosystems under cultivation in these regions would have been affected by environmental conditions and by abandonment or neglect during mass migrations, which normally do not occur unless people are fleeing from starvation or drought. An Aztec legend that recounts the god Quetzalcoatl's flight from his once-splendid Tula indicate such a period of disaster; this seems to be the first recorded instance of deforestation and the resulting effect on cacao orchards:[28] "Quetzalcoatl, who already was troubled, who already was saddened, was thereupon minded to go, to abandon his city of Tula. Thereupon he made ready. It is said that he had everything burned, his house of gold, his house of seashells; and still other Toltec crafts, objects which were marvelous achievements, which were costly achievements, he buried, all; he hid all there in difficult places, perhaps inside a mountain or in a canyon. And also the cacao trees he changed into mesquites."[29]

What distinguishes the deforestation occurring today from that of more-ancient times, however, is the relatively unprecedented, escalating rate at which forests are disappearing within our lifetime. For instance, Central American countries—all ancient growers of cacao (Belize, Costa Rica, El Salvador, Guatemala, Honduras, Nicaragua, and Panama)—have experienced alarming rates of deforestation, especially since 1950. Approximately one-third of their forests is all that remains.[30] Although the rate of deforestation seems to be slowing, it is still alarming. According to the Food and Agriculture Organization of the United Nations, 285,000 hectares (704,250 square acres or 1,100 square miles) of deforestation occurred each year in Central America between 2000 and 2005. Guatemala alone, between 1990 and 2005, lost 14.1 percent of its total forest habitat, and Honduras, 37 percent in the same time period. Mexico, which in the mid-1980s lost 800,000 hectares annually (1,976,840 acres or 3,088 square miles), continued to lose almost 7 percent of its forests between 1990 and 2005. Placed within a worldwide context, we see a situation of unparalleled magnitude: over 125,000,000 hectares of deforestation occurred between 1990 and 2005, an area slightly larger than Texas, California, and New York combined.[31] What does this mean in terms of the heart and soul of the planet?

global warming: chocolate captures carbon

Although industrial processes have contributed to a majority of gas emissions released into the atmosphere, deforestation during the last half of the twentieth century also corresponded with measurable increases in global warming. The increasingly precise sampling techniques now available indicate that global warming has increased dramatically within the last three decades, with 2005 being the hottest year on record.[32] (These startling facts are further supported by ice core samples that verify that 2005 also had a 27 percent greater concentration of atmospheric CO_2 than any year within the last 650,000 years.)[33] A clear correlation seems to exist between a rise in greenhouse gases and global climate changes. The challenge lies in determining how greenhouse gas emissions can be modified.

One way is through regenerated forests. Tropical rainforests are important sources of carbon sinks that capture or sequester carbon dioxide and greenhouse gas emissions. As a shade-grown crop, the cacao tree and a hectare of its surrounding forest

Figure 6.12   A co-op owner affiliated with Green and Black's organic cacao orchards in the Toledo District of Belize.

system can store or capture twenty to one hundred times more carbon dioxide than an equal area of farmland or pasture.[34]

Intensive cacao cultivation during the nineteenth and twentieth centuries shifted cacao away from a shaded forested environment to a monoculture, shadeless, plantation system in which only one or two species, such as banana, were planted with the cacao tree. This lack of biodiversity encouraged pests and fungi that otherwise were kept at bay by a host of other microbes. As a result, a vicious cycle of pesticide use and chemical fertilizers became necessary, further eliminating a functioning ecosystem of microbes, insects, plants, trees, and animals.[35] Even more important, these shadeless plantation systems removed forest cover from the surface of the earth that once actively captured carbon dioxide and other greenhouse gases from the atmosphere.

Today, chocolate companies are reevaluating their approach and are investing in small, independently owned cacao orchards within Central America that use rustic management systems. Here, cacao is grown under a canopy of tropical forest cover where select forest trees have been thinned to allow more filtered light. This encourages the most biologically diverse environment while retaining the forest's ability to act as a carbon sink for atmospheric gases.

We were able to appreciate this system firsthand while visiting organic cacao operations during our filming in the Toledo District of Belize (fig. 6.12). Here, encouraged

by the policies between local cacao growers and Green and Black's chocolate company of England, organic cacao grows interspersed within a thinned, layered, shaded canopy of forest trees, mimicking the way it was cultivated in ancient times. The forest canopy performs the functions of chemical fertilizers and pesticides in providing nutrients to the soil, preventing disease, and increasing the longevity of the cacao tree. This system has also promoted economic freedom and improved living conditions among smallholder cacao farmers—the twenty-first-century cacaoteros—as Green and Black's has guaranteed them a constant price for their organic cacao.

It is fitting that efforts today to save the rainforests and the species inhabiting them can be hinged on the natural viability of a subcanopy of agricultural trees such as cacao, a once-proud member of a diverse forested ecosystem that had, for millennia, supported animals and humans alike. Words from a community leader in Coban, Guatemala, in 2004 summed up this ideal beautifully as he addressed an audience of Q'eqchi Maya who were holding painted calabash cups of chocolate in their hands: "Our navels are stuck to the earth." The ancient Mesoamericans understood this. Like the Maya deity who nurtures a cacao pod through his "cosmic" center (fig. 6.13), we too are linked to cacao and its vital role in balancing our fragile planet.

Figure 6.13 (opposite)   A cacao god with a split cacao pod growing from his navel. (Late Classic Maya figurine)

Notes

~~~~~~~~~~~~~~

1 chocolate and the supernatural realm

1. Tedlock 1996:63, 64.
2. Ibid., 63.
3. Ibid., 103.
4. This god is not the same as the Maya deity Ek Chuah, the Postclassic patron of cacao growers and merchants, discussed in chapter 2.
5. Chinchilla Mazariegos 2005:15.
6. VanKirk and Bassett-VanKirk 1996:6.
7. Codex Nuttall 1975:47.
8. Tedlock 1996:17.
9. Ibid., 146.
10. Coe and Coe 1996:42. Although many scholars, using other passages, have concluded that corn was the sole ingredient that formed humans, Sophie Coe and Michael Coe seem to suggest that all the foods from Split Place Mountain were used.
11. Tedlock 1996:73.
12. Peterson 1990:52.
13. Freidel et al. 1993:118.
14. Tedlock 1996:106.
15. Girard 1979.
16. Freidel et al. 1993:53.
17. Ibid., 118.
18. Peterson 1990:14.
19. Ibid., 16.
20. Taube 1998:446–47.
21. Freidel et al. 1993:454.
22. Examples are the Chilam Balams of Mani, Kaua, and Chumayel. See Milbrath 1999:70. In the Maya creation story depicted by the Chilam Balam of Chumayel, four cosmic trees, each assigned a different directional color and bird, delineate the cardinal directions while a fifth, the ceiba tree, or the Yax Imix Che, is at the center. Maya and Mixtec pictorial manuscripts also depict directional trees with a central fifth tree.
23. Aveni 1983:156–57.
24. Von Winning 1985:50–51, 74.
25. Schele and Freidel 1990:223–24.
26. Codex Tro-Cortesianus (Madrid Codex) 1967.
27. Tedlock 1996:99.
28. Ibid., 85.
29. Paxton 2001:58.
30. Barnhart 1996:16.
31. Freidel et al. 1993:410–12n19.
32. Miller and Taube 1997:146.
33. Freidel et al. 1993:194.
34. Miller and Taube 1997:80.
35. For a similar vase see Coe 1982:76.

2 chocolate and ritual in mesoamerica

1. Bunzel 1952:44.
2. MacNeish 1983:127.
3. Steele 1997:2.
4. Stone 1995:20.
5. Keith Prufer, personal communication, 2001.
6. Willard 1926:230–31.
7. Cacao trees in Yucatan have been documented growing in cenotes. See Gómez-Pompa et al. 1990:251; Young 1994:23.
8. Miller and Taube 1997:104.
9. Thompson 1956:107. See also Barrera Vásquez et al. 1991:32.
10. Thompson 1956:107.
11. Parsons 1991.
12. Taladoire 2001:107. The genesis of ballcourt architecture has often been attributed to the Olmecs along the gulf coast, but Taladoire suggests that the earliest known ballcourt is on the Pacific coast at Paso de la Amada.

13. Day 2001:75–76.

14. Fox 1991:232.

15. This scene may represent a pre-ballgame ritual in which the ballplayer receives magical instructions from his spiritual advisors. Parsons 1969:101–2.

16. Nadal 2001:30.

17. Thompson 1956:101.

18. Millon 1955:163.

19. Rice 2004:249.

20. Boone 2000:95–96.

21. Coggins 2002:64–66. Coggins makes an interesting case for the resemblance of the cacao and fire glyphs.

22. Thompson 1990:297.

23. Stanzione 2003:266.

24. Ibid., 158.

25. Young 1994:22–23. This wild form of cacao is a climbing tree or shrub with pods similar to the five-ridged criollo variety but with ten ridges.

26. McGee 1990:ix.

27. Freidel et al. 1993:215–16.

28. McGee 1990:46.

29. Davis 1978:73.

30. Marjil de Jesus et al. 1984:16.

31. Tozzer 1907:140.

32. Davis 1978:213–14.

33. Girard 1962:92–93.

34. Páez Betancor and Arboleda 1965:269.

35. Fowler 1989:239–40. Volador ceremonies in Mesoamerica symbolize the erection of the cosmic tree (pole) in which the Underworld, Earth, and Sky are joined into a cosmic unity.

36. The month of Muan would have fallen within the Gregorian calendar months of April and May, which was cacao harvest time from the 1550s through the 1570s, the decades of Landa's appointments

as a superior and (later) second bishop of Yucatan.

37. Landa 1978:79.

38. Boone 2000:56.

39. Thompson 1956:105.

40. Bunzel 1952:25.

41. Pacheco 1988:30–32.

42. García de Palacio 1985:43.

43. Thompson 1956:104–5.

44. Tulley 2000:2.

45. Landa 1941:102.

46. Ibid., 105.

47. Durán 1971:132.

48. Powis et al. 2002:98.

49. Stuart 1988.

50. Hall et al. 1990.

51. Keith Prufer, personal communication, 2001.

52. Boone 2000:119.

53. George O. Jackson, personal communication, May 2006.

54. Carmichael and Sayer 1992:28.

3 Power, Wealth, and Greed

The chapter epigraph is from Coe and Coe 1996:86. This is their translation of a story recounted by the chronicler Cervantes de Salazar.

1. Coe and Coe 1996:85.

2. Staines Cicero 2001:389.

3. Carrasco and Hull 2002:26–27.

4. Miller and Martin 2004:75.

5. Ibid., 76. Vases K5359 and K1560 at www.mayavase.com show that God L's possessions are confiscated by the moon goddess and her rabbit companion and that the maize god in three scenes taunts and kicks a naked God L.

6. Coe and Coe 1996:19.

7. Millon 1955:175–76.

8. Fowler 1989:108–10.

9. Gómez-Pompa et al. 1990.

10. Landa 1941:164.

11. Landa 1966:230.

12. Kepecs and Boucher 1996:78.

13. Sheets 2002:9–10.

14. Ibid., 20.

15. Powis et al. 2007.

16. For the Ulua Valley sherds, see Henderson et al. 2007: 18937–18940; for the Colha vessels, see Powis et al. 2002:97–98.

17. Chase and Chase 1989:21–32.

18. Berlo 1980:327–29.

19. Bove and Busto 2003:51, 73.

20. Berlo 1980:327–29. Another interesting example from Lago Amatitlan is a censer lid with a quetzal perched on top of a pile of cacao pods. On the cylinder supports of the censer, cacao imagery appears as pods growing from curly, leafy vines, resembling the monuments at El Baúl in the Cotzumalhuapa art. Ibid., 269.

21. Taube 2003a.

22. Carlson 1991:fig. 9e.

23. Ibid., 44–46.

24. Ibid., 60.

25. Scholes and Roys 1968:3, 316–17.

26. Landa 1966:94–95n415.

27. Millon 1955:150.

28. Ibid., 151, citing p. 292 of *Vita di Cristoforo Colombo, descritta da Ferdinando, e tradotta da Alfonso Ulloa* (London 1867).

29. Scholes and Roys 1968:4.

30. Henderson 1981:65.

31. Ibid., 67, 216, 222.

32. McAnany 1995:133–35.

33. Miller 1997:35–37.

34. Houston 1997.

35. Freidel et al. 1993:236; Miller 1997:35.

36. Sahagún 1959:9:1.

37. Durán 1994:247–62.

38. Townsend 1992:195.

39. Sahagún 1970:1:41.

40. Sahagún 1959:9:1.

41. Sahagún 1970:1:42.

42. Millon 1955:139–41.

43. Gasco 1996:4, 2.

44. Landa 1966:95n417.

45. Gasco 1996:4.

46. Landa 1966:95n417.

47. Bove et al. 1993:187.

48. Scholes and Roys 1968:323, 328.

49. The Nahuatl-speaking Pipils of Cotzumalguapa and Escuintla and the Tz'utujil Mayas were allied against the Quiché and Kaqchikel Mayas.

50. Stanzione 2003:214.

51. Orellana 1995:41.

52. Stanzione 2003:179.

53. Orellana 1995:80–83.

54. Stanzione 2003:194.

4 serve up the chocolate

The chapter epigraph is from Sahagún 1979:8:39–40.

1. The accounts include those by Sahagún, Landa, Oviedo y Valdés, and others.

2. Roys 1933:95–96.

3. Baer and Merrifield 1971:209–10.

4. Boot 2005:17.

5. Reents-Budet 1994:127.

6. Ibid., 2–66.

7. Henderson et al. 2007:18937–18940.

8. Powis et al. 2002: 99–100.

9. McNeil 2005.

10. Reents-Budet 1994:79.

11. Barbara McCleod was the first to refer to these descriptions as "recipes," in 1990. The maize-tree glyph is from Stu-art 2005:133; the frothy cacao glyph is from Reents-Budet 1994:206.

12. Christina Luke, e-mail correspondence, 2005.

13. Schaffer 1992.

14. Luke 2002; Luke et al. 2002.

15. Justin Kerr, personal communication, November 2005.

16. Reents-Budet 1994:80, 86.

17. McNeil 2005.

18. Gerstle and Sheets 2002:78.

19. Schmidt et al. 1998:630.

20. McNeil 2005.

21. Reents-Budet 1994:358.

22. Coe and Kerr 1997:97.

23. Lacadena Garcia-Gallo 2003:42.

5 The Healing Powers of chocolate

The chapter epigraph is from Roys 1965:6.

1. Tedlock 1996:92.

2. Roys 1965:37. See also Gubler and Bolles 2000; Roys 1933.

3. Gubler and Bolles 2000:132, 149.

4. Lopez Austin 1988:53–59; Roys 1965:xi.

5. Durán 1994:244–45.

6. Coe and Coe 1996:122.

7. Ibid., 123.

8. Dillinger et al. 2000:2061S.

9. Coe 1994:54, citing Oviedo y Valdés, *Historia General y Natural de las Indias* (1959 reprint).

10. Sahagún 1963:11:112, 170, 176.

11. Ibid., 189, 12. The three additives were *Cymbopetalum penduliflorum* (earflower), *Piper sanctum* (root beer plant), and *Vanilla planifolia* (vanilla).

12. Pastino 2007.

13. Durán 1964:266.

14. Coe 1994:55.

15. Apgar and Tarka 1999; Benton 1999.

16. Dillinger et al. 2000:2064S, citing Santiago de Valverdes Turices, *Un discurso del chocolate*, published in Seville in 1624.

17. Coe and Coe 1996:94.

18. Waizel Bucay and Torres-Cabrera 2002:31.

19. Faust 1998:603–42.

20. Montgomery 1995:65–69.

21. Lothrop 1926:56.

22. Tomaso et al. 1996.

23. Knight 1999:143–52.

24. Würsch and Finot 1999.

25. Kritchevsky 1999.

26. Lee et al. 2003:7295.

27. Fisher et al. 2003:2281.

6 Balancing the cosmos

The chapter epigraph is from Yoon 1998.

1. Freidel et al. 1993:85–89. During its evening journey, with a voided cleft, or "jaws," pointed downward, the Milky Way was possibly imagined by early Maya as an inverted cayman.

2. Milbrath 1999:76.

3. Lara 1996:38–41.

4. Schmidt 2003:fig. 54.

5. Roys 1933:100.

6. Taube 2003b:484.

7. Cacao trees need a minimum of 1,000 millimeters (40 inches) of rain per year and cannot survive in extended dry periods. Millon 1955:15–17.

8. Potts 1996:50.

9. Christenson 2003:143n329. The term *canté* derives from *k'an té* or *q'an té*, with *k'an/q'an* meaning "yellow" and *té* meaning "tree."

10. Roys 1933:99.

11. Young 1994:112.

12. Ibid., 98.

13. Ibid., 11.

14. Pacheco et al. 1996.

15. Munoz et al. 2003.

16. Presilla 2001:15–16.

17. Young 1994:163.

18. Dahlins 1979:31.

19. Fowler 1989:108–9.

20. Kaplan 2006:4.

21. Stanzione 2003:78.

22. Bergmann 1969:90.

23. Gasco 1987:161.

24. Ibid.

25. Pohl et al. 1996:358.

26. Davis 2005.

27. Mathews 2002:89.

28. Gill 2000:381, 122, 123.

29. Sahagún 1978:3:33.

30. Gómez et al. 1997.

31. For data on the extent of losses of forest ecosystems, see Food and Agriculture Organization 2006; Gómez et al. 1997.

32. Hansen et al. 2006. Global warming is now calculated as having increased by 0.6°C during the past three decades—a notable escalation compared to the total increase of 0.8°C for the entire twentieth century. According to the Goddard Institute for Space Studies, 2005 was perhaps the warmest year ever recorded, a remarkable event because (unlike in 1998) there was no El Niño to boost the temperatures. Most of this warming took place in the northern latitudes of the Arctic region.

33. Brook 2005.

34. International Cacao Organization 2000.

35. Diamond 2003.

bibliography

Apgar, Joan L., and Stanley M. Tarka Jr.

1999   Methylxanthines. In Knight, *Chocolate and Cocoa*, 153–73.

Aveni, Anthony F.

1983   *Skywatchers of Ancient Mexico*. Austin: University of Texas Press.

Baer, Phillip, and William R. Merrifield

1971   *Two Studies on the Lacandones of Mexico*. Norman: Summer Institute of Linguistics of the University of Oklahoma.

Barnhart, Edwin Lawrence

1996   A Report on the First Twenty-three Pages of Dresden Codex and Xochicalco: An Ancient Ceremonial Site in the State of Morelos, Mexico. Masters thesis, University of Texas at Austin.

Barrera Vásquez, Alfredo, Juan Ramón Bastarrachea Manzano, William Brito Sansores, Refugio Vermont Salas, David Dzul Góngora, and Domingo Dzul Poot

1991   *Diccionario Maya: Maya-Español, Español-Maya*. 2nd ed. Mexico City: Editorial Porrúa.

Benton, David

1999   Chocolate Craving: Biological or Psychological Phenomenon? In Knight, *Chocolate and Cocoa*, 256–78.

Bergmann, John F.

1969   The Distribution of Cacao Cultivation in Pre-Columbian America. *Annals of the Association of American Geographers* 59:85–96.

Berlo, Janet Catherine

1980   Teotihuacan Art Abroad: A Study of Metropolitan Style and Provincial Transformation in Incensario Workshops. Ph.D. dissertation, Yale University.

1984   *Teotihuacan Art Abroad: A Study of Metropolitan Style and Provincial Transformation in Incensario Workshops*. 2 vols. BAR International Series 199. Oxford, UK: British Archaeological Reports.

Berrin, Kathleen, ed.

1988   *Feathered Serpents and Flowering Trees: Reconstructing the Murals of Teotihuacán*. Seattle: Fine Arts Museums of San Francisco and University of Washington Press.

Boone, Elizabeth Hill

2000   *Stories in Red and Black: Pictorial Histories of the Aztecs and Mixtecs*. Austin: University of Texas Press.

Boot, Erik

2005   A Preliminary Overview of Common and Uncommon Classic Maya Vessel Type Collocations in the Primary Standard Sequence. http://www.mayavase.com/essays/ boot26vesseltypes.

Bove, Frederick J., and Sonia Medrano Busto

2003   Teotihuacan, Militarism, and Pacific Guatemala. In Braswell, *Maya and Teotihuacan*, 45–79.

Bove, Frederick J., Sonia Medrano B., Brenda Lou P., and Barbara Arroyo L., eds.

1993   The Balberta Project: *The Terminal Formative–Early Classic Transition on the Pacific Coast of Guatemala*. University of

Pittsburgh Memoirs in Latin America Archaeology 6. Pittsburgh: University of Pittsburgh, Department of Anthropology; Guatemala: Asociación Tikal.

Braswell, Geoffrey F., ed.

2003   *The Maya and Teotihuacan: Reinterpreting Early Classic Interaction.* Austin: University of Texas Press.

Brook, Edward J.

2005   Tiny Bubbles Tell All. *Science* 310 (5752): 1285–87.

Bunzel, Ruth

1952   *Chichicastenango: A Guatemalan Village.* Locust Valley, NY: J. J. Augustin.

Carlson, John B.

1991   *Venus-Regulated Warfare and Ritual Sacrifice in Mesoamerica: Teotihuacan and the Cacaxtla "Star Wars" Connection.* Center for Archaeoastronomy Technical Publication 7. College Park: University of Maryland.

Carmichael, Elizabeth, and Chloë Sayer

1992   *The Skeleton at the Feast: The Day of the Dead in Mexico.* Austin: University of Texas Press.

Carrasco, Michael D., and Kerry Hull

2002   The Cosmogonic Symbolism of the Corbeled Vault in Maya Architecture. *Mexicon* 24 (2): 26–32.

Chase, Diane Z., and Arlen F. Chase

1989   Routes of Trade and Communication and the Integration of Maya Society: The Vista from Santa Rita Corozal. In *Coastal Maya Trade and Exchange*, edited by Heather McKillop and Paul Healy, 19–32. Occasional Papers in Anthropology no. 8. Petersborough, ON: Trent University.

Chinchilla Mazariegos, Oswaldo

2005   Dioses y dosas del cacao. In *Kakaw: El chocolate en la cultura de Guatemala*, edited by Oswaldo Chinchilla Mazariegos, 13–19. Guatemala: Museo Popol Vuh, Universidad Francisco Marroquin.

Christenson, Allen J.

2003   *Popol Vuh: The Sacred Book of the Maya.* Winchester, UK: O Books.

Codex Borgia

1976   *Codex Borgia: Biblioteca Apostolica Vaticana (Messicano Riserva 28).* Commentary by Karl A. Nowotny. Graz, Austria: Akademische Druck-u. Verlagsanstalt.

Codex Dresden

1886   *Erläuterungen zur Mayahandschrift der Königlichen öffentlichen Bibliothek zu Dresden.* Commentary by Ernst Wilhelm Förstemann. Dresden: Warnatz and Lehmann.

Codex Féjérvary-Mayer

1971   *Codex Féjérvary-Mayer.* Introduction by C. A. Burland. Graz, Austria: Akademische Druck-u. Verlagsanstalt.

Codex Nuttall

1902   *Codex Nuttall: Facsimile of an Ancient Mexican Codex Belonging to Lord Zouche of Harynworth, England.* Introduction by Zelia Nuttall. Cambridge, MA: Peabody Museum of American Archaeology and Ethnology, Harvard University.

1975   *The Codex Nuttall: A Picture Manuscript from Ancient Mexico: The Peabody Museum Facsimile.* Edited by Zelia Nuttall. New York: Dover Publications.

Codex Rios

1900   *Il Manuscritto Messicano Vaticano 3738, Detto il Codice Rios.* Rome: Danesi.

Codex Tro-Cortesianus (Madrid Codex)

1967   *Codex Tro-Cortesianus, Museo de América, Madrid.* Introduction by Ferdinand Anders. Graz, Austria: Akademische Druck-u. Verlagsanstalt.

Codex Tudela

1980   *Códice Tudela.* Introduction by Donald Robertson and summary by Wigberto Jimenez Morena. Madrid: Ediciones Culturales Hispánica del Instituto de Cooperación Iberoamericana.

Codex Vindobonensis

1963   *Codex Vindobonensis Mexicanus 1, Osterreichische National-bibliothek Wien.* Graz, Austria: Akademische Druck-u Verlagsanstalt.

Coe, Michael D.

1982   *Old Gods and Young Heroes: The Pearlman Collection of Maya Ceramics.* Jerusalem: Israel Museum, Maremont Pavilion of Ethnic Arts.

Coe, Michael D., and Justin Kerr

1997   *The Art of the Maya Scribe.* London: Thames and Hudson.

Coe, Michael D., and Rex Koontz

2002　*Mexico: From the Olmecs to the Aztecs.* 5th ed. New York: Thames and Hudson.

Coe, Sophie D.

1994　*America's First Cuisines.* Austin: University of Texas Press.

Coe, Sophie D., and Michael D. Coe

1996　*The True History of Chocolate.* New York: Thames and Hudson.

Coggins, Clemency

2002　Toltec. *Res: Anthropology and Aesthetics* 42:34–85.

Cruz, Martín de la

1940　*The Badianus Manuscript (Codex Barberini, Latin 241), Vatican Library: An Aztec Herbal of 1552.* Translated by Emily Walcott Emmart. Baltimore, MD: Johns Hopkins Press.

Dahlins, Bruce H.

1979　Cropping Cash in the Protoclassic: A Cultural Impact Statement. In *Maya Archaeology and Ethnohistory*, edited by Norman Hammond and Gordon R. Willey, 21–37. Austin: University of Texas Press.

Davis, Bob

2005　In Guatemala: A Battle over Logs and a Lost Kingdom. *Wall Street Journal*, November 12–13.

Davis, Virginia Dale

1978　Ritual of the Northern Lacandon Maya. Ph.D. dissertation, Tulane University, New Orleans.

Day, Jane Stevenson

2001　Performing on the Court. In Whittington, *Sport of Life and Death*, 65–77.

Diamond, Jared

2003　The Last Americans: Environmental Collapse and the End of Civilization. *Harper's Magazine* (June): 43–51.

Dillinger, Teresa L., Patricia Barriga, Sylvia Escárcega, Martha Jimenez, Diana Salazar Lowe, and Louis E. Grivetti

2000　Food of the Gods: A Cure for Humanity? A Cultural History of the Medicinal and Ritual Use of Chocolate. *Journal of Nutrition* 130:2057S–2072S.

Durán, Diego

1964　*The Aztecs: The History of the Indies of New Spain.* Trans-

lated, with notes, by Fernando Horcasitas and Doris Heyden. New York: Orion Press.

1971　*Book of the Gods and Rites and the Ancient Calendar.* Translated, with notes, by Doris Heyden and Fernando Horcasitas. Norman: University of Oklahoma Press.

1994　*The History of the Indies of New Spain.* Translated, annotated, and with an introduction by Doris Heyden. Norman: University of Oklahoma Press.

Faust, Betty Bernice

1998　Cacao Beans and Chili Peppers: Gender Socialization in the Cosmology of a Yucatec Maya Curing Ceremony. *Sex Roles: A Journal of Research* 39 (7/8): 603–42.

Fisher, Naomi D. L., Meghan Hughes, Marie Gerhard-Herman, and Norman K. Hollenberg

2003　Flavonol-Rich Cocoa Induces Nitric-Oxide Dependent Vasodilation in Healthy Humans. *Journal of Hypertension* 21 (12): 2281–86.

Food and Agriculture Organization (FAO) and Global Forest Resources Assessment (FRA) of the United Nations

2006　FRA 2005 Global Tables: Change in Extent of Forest and Other Wooded Land 1990–2005. www.fao.org/forestry/site/32033/en.

Fowler, William R.

1989　*The Cultural Evolution of Ancient Nahua Civilizations: The Pipil-Nicarao of Central America.* Norman: University of Oklahoma Press.

Fox, John W.

1991　The Lords of Light versus the Lords of Dark: The Postclassic Highland Maya Ballgame. In Scarborough and Wilcox, *The Mesoamerican Ballgame*, 213–38.

Freidel, David A., Linda Schele, and Joy Parker

1993　*Maya Cosmos: Three Thousand Years on the Shaman's Path.* New York: William Morrow.

García de Palacio, Diego

1985　*Letter to the King of Spain: Being a Description of the Ancient Provinces of Guazacapan, Izalco, Cuscatlan, and Chiquimula, in the Audiencia of Guatemala, . . .* Translated, with notes, by Ephraim G. Squier. Culver City, CA: Labyrinthos.

Garver, John B., cartographer

1989　The Ancient Maya World (map). *National Geographic*

Magazine 176, no. 4. Washington DC: National Geographic Society.

Gasco, Janine L.

1987   Cacao and the Economic Integration of Native Society in Colonial Soconusco, New Spain. Ph.D. dissertation, University of California at Santa Barbara.

1996   Cacao as Commodity in Postclassic Soconusco. Paper presented at the annual meeting of the American Anthropological Association, San Francisco, November.

Gerstle, Andrea I., and Payson Sheets

2002   Structure 4: A Storehouse-Workshop for Household 4. In *Before the Volcano Erupted: The Ancient Ceren Village in Central America*, edited by Payson Sheets, 74–80. Austin: University of Texas Press.

Gill, Richardson B.

2000   *The Great Maya Droughts: Water, Life and Death.* Albuquerque: University of New Mexico Press.

Girard, Rafael

1962   *Los Mayas Eternos.* Mexico City: Antigua Librería Robredo.

1979   *Esotericism of the Popol Vuh.* Translated by Blair A. Moffett. Pasadena, CA: Theosophical University Press Online Edition. http://www.theosociety.org/pasadena/popolvuh/pv-hp.htm.

Gómez, Luis Diego, Juan Carlos Godoy, Olga Herrera-MacBryde, and Jose Villa-Lobos

1997   Central America Regional Overview. In *Centres of Plant Diversity: A Guide and Strategy for Their Conservation*, vol. 3, The Americas, edited by S. D. Davis, V. H. Heywood, O. Herrera-MacBryde, J. Villa-Lobos, and A. Hamilton. Cambridge, UK: IUCN Publications Unit. http://www.nmnh.si.edu/botany/projects/cpd.

Gómez-Pompa, Arturo, José Salvador Flores, and Mario Aliphat Fernández

1990   The Sacred Cacao Groves of the Maya. *Latin American Antiquity* 1 (3): 247–57.

Gubler, Ruth, and David Bolles, eds.

2000   *The Book of Chilam Balam of Na: Facsimile, Translation and Edited Text.* Lancaster, CA: Labyrinthos.

Hall, Grant D., Stanley M. Tarka Jr., W. Jeffrey Hurst, David Stuart, and Richard E. W. Adams

1990   Cacao Residues in Ancient Maya Vessels from Rio Azul, Guatemala. *American Antiquity* 55 (1): 138–43.

Hansen, J., R. Ruedy, M. Sato, and K. Lo

2006   Global Temperature Trends: 2005 Summation. GISS Surface Temperature Analysis. Goddard Institute for Space Studies, NASA. http://data.giss.nasa.gov/gistemp/2005.

Henderson, John S.

1981   *The World of the Ancient Maya.* Ithaca, NY: Cornell University Press.

Henderson, John S., Rosemary A. Joyce, Gretchen R. Hall, W. Jeffrey Hurst, and Patrick E. McGovern

2007   *Proceedings of the National Academy of Sciences of the USA* 104:18937–18940.

Houston, Stephen D.

1997   A King Worth a Hill of Beans. *Archaeology* 50 (3): 40.

International Cacao Organization (ICCO)

2000   What Is the Carbon Sequestration Value of *Theobroma Cacao?* 9 August. www.icco.org/questions/carbon.htm.

Joyce, Rosemary A., and John S. Henderson

2001   Beginnings of Village Life in Eastern Mesoamerica. *Latin American Antiquity* 12 (1): 5–23.

Kampen, Michael Edwin

1972   *The Sculptures of El Tajín, Veracruz, Mexico.* Gainesville: University of Florida Press.

Kaplan, Jonathan

2006   Guatemala's Ancient Maya: Expedition Briefing. http://www.earthwatch.org/atf/cf/%7BBD9A05BF-0860-451E-AA86-7FBF37574C00%7D/KAPLAN_BRIEFING.PDF.

Kepecs, Susan, and Sylviane Boucher

1996   The Pre-Hispanic Cultivation of Rejolladas and Stone-Lands: New Evidence from Northeast Yucatan. In *The Managed Mosaic: Ancient Maya Agriculture and Resource Use*, edited by Scott L. Fedick, 69–91. Salt Lake City: University of Utah Press.

Kerr, Justin

n.d.   Maya Vase Database: An Archive of Rollout Photographs. FAMSI. http://research.famsi.org/kerrmaya.html.

n.d.   A Precolumbian Portfolio: An Archive of Photographs.

FAMSI Research Materials. http://research.famsi.org/kerrportfolio.html.

Kingsborough, Edward

1831 *Antiquities of Mexico: Comprising Fac-Similes of Ancient Mexican Paintings and Hieroglyphics, . . .* Vol. 3. London: Robert Havell and Colnaghi, Son, and Company.

Knight, Ian

1999 Minerals in Cocoa and Chocolate. In Knight, *Chocolate and Cocoa*, 143–52.

Knight, Ian, ed.

1999 *Chocolate and Cocoa: Health and Nutrition.* London: International Cocoa Organization; Malden, MA: Blackwell Science; with the International Cocoa Research and Education Foundation.

Kritchevsky, David

1999 Cocoa Butter and Constituent Fatty Acids. In Knight, *Chocolate and Cocoa*, 79–86.

Lacadena Garcia-Gallo, Alfonso

2003 *The Glyphic Corpus from Ek'Balam, Yucatán, México.* Translated by Alex Lomónaco. http://www.famsi.org/reports.

Landa, Diego de

1941 *Landa's Relación de las Cosas de Yucatan.* Translated and edited, with notes, by Alfred M. Tozzer. Papers of the Peabody Museum of Archaeology and Ethnology, Harvard University 18. Cambridge, MA: Peabody Museum.

1966 *Landa's Relación de las Cosas de Yucatan.* Translated and edited, with notes, by Alfred M. Tozzer. Reprint, New York: Kraus.

1978 *Yucatan before and after the Conquest.* Translated, with notes, by William Gates. New York: Dover Publications.

Lara, Ankarino Sibbing

1996 The Sculpted Stone Vessels of Copán, Honduras: A Stylistic, Iconographic, and Textual Analysis of the Saklaktuns. Senior thesis, Harvard University.

Lazzarini, L., ed.

2002 *Asmosia VI: Interdisciplinary Studies on Ancient Stone: Proceedings of the Sixth International Conference of the Association for the Study of Marble and Other Stones in Antiquity, Venice, June 15–18, 2000.* Venice,

Italy: Bottega d'Erasmo Aldo Ausilio Editore (Padova).

Lee, Ki Won, Young Jun Kim, Hyong Joo Lee, and Chang Yong Lee

2003 Cocoa Has More Phenolic Phytochemicals and a Higher Antioxidant Capacity than Teas and Red Wine. *Journal of Agricultural and Food Chemistry* 51:7292–95.

Linné, Sigvald

1942 *Mexican Highland Cultures: Archaeological Researches at Teotihuacan, Calpulalpan and Chalchicomula in 1934/35.* Stockholm: Statens Etnografiska Museum.

Lopez Austin, Alfredo

1988 *The Human Body and Ideology: Concepts of the Ancient Nahuas.* Translated by Thelma and Bernard Ortiz de Montellano. Salt Lake City: University of Utah Press.

Lothrop, Samuel K.

1926 *Pottery of Costa Rica and Nicaragua.* 2 vols. New York: Heye Foundation, Museum of the American Indian.

Luke, Christina

2002 Mesoamerican White Stone Vase Traditions and the Use of Color. In Lazzarini, *Asmosia VI*, 507–16.

Luke, Christina, Rosemary A. Joyce, John S. Henderson, and Robert H. Tykot

2002 Stone Vase Traditions in Mesoamerica: A Case from Honduras. In Lazzarini, *Asmosia VI*, 485–96.

MacNeish, Richard S.

1983 Mesoamerica. In *Early Man in the New World*, edited by Richard Shutler Jr., 123–35. Beverly Hills, CA: Sage Publications.

Marcus, Joyce, and Kent V. Flannery

1996 *Zapotec Civilization: How Urban Society Evolved in Mexico's Oaxaca Valley.* New York: Thames and Hudson.

Marjil de Jesus, Antonio, Lazaro de Mazariegos, and Blas Guillen

1984 *A Spanish Manuscript Letter on the Lacandones in the Archives of the Indies at Seville.* Translated, with notes, by Alfred M. Tozzer. Additional notes by Frank E. Comparato. Culver City, CA: Labyrinthos.

Martin, Simon

2006 Cacao in Ancient Maya Religion: First Fruit from the Maize

Tree and Other Tales from the Underworld. In *Chocolate in Mesoamerica: A Cultural History of Cacao*, edited by Cameron McNeil, 154–183. Gainesville: University Press of Florida.

Mathews, Ruth A. Shavers

2002   Geology, Environment, and Lime Production Variation in the Maya Lowlands. Masters thesis, University of Texas at San Antonio.

McAnany, Patricia A.

1995   *Living with the Ancestors: Kinship and Kingship in Ancient Maya Society*. Austin: University of Texas Press.

McGee, R. Jon

1990   *Life, Ritual, and Religion among the Lacandon Maya*. Belmont, CA: Wadsworth.

McNeil, Cameron L.

2005   Food of the Ancestors: Cacao Use and Iconography at Copan, Honduras. Paper presented at Maya Chocolate and Precious Delights: The 23rd Annual Maya Weekend, University of Pennsylvania Museum of Archaeology and Anthropology, Philadelphia, April 9.

McNeil, Cameron L., ed.

2006   *Chocolate in Mesoamerica: A Cultural History of Cacao*. Gainesville: University Press of Florida.

Milbrath, Susan

1999   *Star Gods of the Maya: Astronomy in Art, Folklore, and Calendars*. Austin: University of Texas Press.

Miller, Mary Ellen

1997   Imaging Maya Art. *Archaeology* 50 (3): 34–40.

1999   *Maya Art and Architecture*. London: Thames and Hudson.

Miller, Mary Ellen, and Simon Martin (Kathleen Berrin, curator)

2004   *Courtly Art of the Ancient Maya*. San Francisco: Fine Arts Museums and New York: Thames and Hudson.

Miller, Mary Ellen, and Karl Taube

1997   *An Illustrated Dictionary of the Gods and Symbols of Ancient Mexico and the Maya*. New York: Thames and Hudson.

Millon, René F.

1955   When Money Grew on Trees: A Study of Cacao in Ancient Mesoamerica. Ph.D. dissertation, Columbia University, New York.

1988   Where Do They All Come From? The Provenance of the Wagner Murals from Teotihuacan. In Berrin, *Feathered Serpents and Flowering Trees*, 78–113.

Montgomery, John Ellis

1995   Sculptors of the Realm: Classic Maya Artists' Signatures and Sculptural Style during the Reign of Piedras Negras Ruler 7. Masters thesis, University of New Mexico at Albuquerque.

Morris, Ann Axtel

1931   Murals from the Temple of the Warriors and Adjacent Structures. In *The Temple of the Warriors at Chichen Itza, Yucatan*, by Earl H. Morris, Ann A. Morris, and Jean Charlot. Carnegie Institution of Washington no. 406. Washington, DC: Carnegie Institution.

Muñoz, David Z., Alejandro Estrada, and Eduardo Naranjo

2003   Primates in Agroecosystems: Cacao Plantations (Comalcalco, Tabasco, Mexico). Laboratorio de Primatología. http://www.primatesmx.com/primcomalcalcoeng.htm.

Nadal, Laura Filloy

2001   Rubber and Rubber Balls in Mesoamerica. In Whittington, *Sport of Life and Death*, 20–31.

Orellana, Sandra L.

1995   *Ethnohistory of the Pacific Coast*. Lancaster, CA: Labyrinthos.

Pacheco, José Fernando, Bret M. Whitney, and Luiz P. Gonzaga

1996   A New Genus and Species of Furnariid (Aves: Furnariidae) from the Cocoa-Growing Region of Southeastern Bahia, Brazil. *Wilson Bulletin* 108 (3): 397–433.

Pacheco, Luis

1988   *Tradiciones y costumbres del Pueblo Maya Kekchi: Noviazgo, matrimonio, secretos, etc.* San José, Costa Rica: Editorial Ambar.

Paez Betancor, Alonso, and Pedro de Arboleda

1965   Descripción de San Bartolomé, del Partido de Atitlán, año 1585. *Anales de la Sociedad de Geografía e Historia* 38:262–76. Guatemala City: La Sociedad de Geografía e Historia.

Parsons, Lee Allen

1969   *Bilbao, Guatemala: An Archaeological Study of the Pacific Coast, Cotzumalhuapa Region*, vol. 2. Publications in Anthropology 12. Milwaukee, WI: Milwaukee Public Museum.

1991   The Ballgame in the Southern Pacific Coast Cotzumal-
       huapa Region and Its Impact on Kaminaljuyu during the
       Middle Classic. In Scarborough and Wilcox, *The Mesoamer-
       ican Ballgame*, 195–212.

Pastino, Blake de

2007   Rare Maya "Death Vase" Discovered. *National Geographic
       News*, December 4. http://news.nationalgeographic.com/
       news/2007/12/071203-maya-vase.html.

Paxton, Merideth

2001   *The Cosmos of the Yucatec Maya: Cycles and Steps from the
       Madrid Codex*. Albuquerque: University of New Mexico
       Press.

Peterson, Jeanette Favrot

1990   *Precolumbian Flora and Fauna: Continuity of Plant and
       Animal Themes in Mesoamerican Art*. San Diego, CA:
       Mingei International Museum of World Folk Art.

Pohl, Mary D., Kevin O. Pope, John G. Jones, John S. Jacob,
       Dolores R. Piperno, Susan D. deFrance, David L. Lentz,
       John A. Gifford, Marie E. Danforth, and J. Kathryn
       Josserand

1996   Early Agriculture in the Maya Lowlands. *Latin American
       Antiquity* 7 (4): 355–72.

Potts, Leanna K.

1996   Chocolate: Past, Present and Future of Cacao. *HerbalGram*
       37:50. Austin: American Botanical Council.

Powis, Terry G., W. Jeffrey Hurst, Maria del Carmen Rodriguez,
       Ponciano Ortiz C., Michael Blake, David Cheetham,
       Michael D. Coe, and John G. Hodgson

2007   Oldest Chocolate in the New World. *Antiquity* 81 (314): np.

Powis, Terry G., Fred Valdez Jr., Thomas R. Hester, W. Jeffrey
       Hurst, and Stanley M. Tarka Jr.

2002   Spouted Vessels and Cacao Use among the Preclassic
       Maya. *Latin American Antiquity* 13 (1): 85–106.

Presilla, Maricel E.

2001   *The New Taste of Chocolate: A Cultural and Natural
       History of Cacao with Recipes*. Berkeley, CA: Ten Speed
       Press.

Reents-Budet, Dorie

1994   *Painting the Maya Universe: Royal Ceramics of the Classic
       Period*. Durham, NC: Duke University Press and Duke
       University Museum of Art.

Relación Geografica de Guaxtepec

1580   *Relaciones Geograficas of Mexico and Guatemala, 1577–1585*.
       Joaquin Garcia Icazbalceta Collection (JGI XXIV-3), Nettie
       Lee Benson Latin American Collection, General Libraries,
       University of Texas–Austin.

Relación Geografica de Teozacoalco

1580   *Relaciones Geograficas of Mexico and Guatemala, 1577–1585*.
       Joaquin Garcia Icazbalceta Collection (JGI XXV-3), Nettie
       Lee Benson Latin American Collection, General Libraries,
       University of Texas–Austin.

Rice, Prudence M.

2004   *Maya Political Science: Time, Astronomy, and the Cosmos*.
       Austin: University of Texas Press.

Roys, Ralph L., trans.

1933   *Book of Chilam Balam of Chumayel*. Washington, DC:
       Carnegie Institution of Washington.

Roys, Ralph L., trans. and ed.

1965   *Ritual of the Bacabs*. Norman: University of Oklahoma
       Press.

Sahagún, Bernardino de

1900? *Historia de las cosas de Nueva España, publicase con fondos de
       la secretaria de instrucción pública y bellas artes de Mexico,
       por Francisco del Paso y Troncoso*. Madrid: Fototipia de
       Hauser y Menet.

1950–1982   *General History of the Things of New Spain:
       Florentine Codex*. Translated and edited by Arthur J. O.
       Anderson and Charles E. Dibble. Monographs of the
       School of American Research 14, parts 1–13. Santa Fe, NM:
       School of American Research; Salt Lake City: University
       of Utah.

Scarborough, Vernon L., and David R. Wilcox, eds.

1991   *The Mesoamerican Ballgame*. Tucson: University of Arizona
       Press.

Schaffer, Anne-Louise

1992   On the Edge of the Maya World. *Archaeology* 45 (2): 50–52.

Schele, Linda

n.d.   Linda Schele Drawings Collection. FAMSI. http://research.
       famsi.org/schele/html (Schele no. 176).

Schele, Linda, and David Freidel

1990   *A Forest of Kings: The Untold Story of the Ancient Maya*. New
       York: Morrow.

Schmidt, Peter J.

2003   *Planos y dibujos para ilustrar el Informe del Proyecto Arqueologico Chichen Itza, Julio 1999 a Diciembre 2002*, vol. 3. Merida: Centro INAH Yucatan.

Schmidt, Peter J., Mercedes de la Garza, and Enrique Nalda, eds.

1998   *Maya*. New York: Rizolli.

Scholes, France V., and Ralph L. Roys

1968   *The Maya Chontal Indians of Acalan-Tixchel: A Contribution to the History and Ethnography of the Yucatan Peninsula.* Norman: University of Oklahoma Press.

Sheets, Payson, ed.

2002   *Before the Volcano Erupted: The Ancient Ceren Village in Central America.* Austin: University of Texas Press.

Staines Cicero, Leticia

2001   Las imágenes pintadas en las tapas de Bóveda. In *La pintura mural prehispánica en México*, vol. 2, *Area Maya*, part 4, compiled by Beatriz de la Fuente, 389–402. Mexico City: Universidad Nacional Autónoma de México, Instituto de Investigaciones Estéticas.

Stanzione, Vincent J.

2003   *Rituals of Sacrifice: Walking the Face of the Earth on the Sacred Path of the Sun: A Journey through the Tz'utujil Maya World of Santiago Atitlán.* Albuquerque: University of New Mexico Press.

Steele, Janet Fitzsimmons

1997   Cave Rituals in Oaxaca, Mexico. Paper presented at the annual meeting of the Society for American Archaeology, Nashville, April.

Stone, Andrea J.

1995   *Images from the Underworld: Naj Tunich and the Tradition of Maya Cave Painting.* 1st ed. Austin: University of Texas Press.

Stuart, David

1988   The Río Azul Cacao Pot: Epigraphic Observations on the Function of a Maya Ceramic Vessel. *Antiquity* 62 (234): 153–57.

Stuart, David, ed.

2005   *Sourcebook for the 29th Maya Hieroglyphic Forum.* The Maya Meetings, March 11–16. Austin: University of Texas.

Taladoire, Eric

2001   The Architectural Background of the Pre-Hispanic Ballgame: An Evolutionary Perspective. In Whittington, *Sport of Life and Death*, 96–115.

Taube, Karl

1998   The Jade Hearth: Centrality, Rulership and the Classic Maya Temple. In *Function and Meaning in Classic Maya Architecture: A Symposium at Dumbarton Oaks, 7th and 8th October 1994*, edited by Stephen D. Houston, 427–78. Washington, DC: Dumbarton Oaks Research Library and Collections.

2003a   Tetitla and the Maya Presence at Teotihuacan. In Braswell, *The Maya and Teotihuacan*, 274–314.

2003b   Ancient and Contemporary Maya Conceptions about Field and Forest. In *The Lowland Maya Area: Three Millennia at the Human-Wildland Interface*, edited by Arturo Gómez-Pompa, Michael F. Allen, Scott L. Fedick, and Juan J. Jimenez-Osorino, 461–92. Binghamton, NY: Food Products Press.

Tedlock, Dennis, translator

1996   *Popol Vuh: The Mayan Book of the Dawn of Life.* New York: Simon and Schuster.

Thompson, J. Eric S.

1956   Notes on the Use of Cacao in Middle America. *Notes on Middle American Archaeology and Ethnology* 128:95–108. Washington, DC: Carnegie Institution.

1990   *Maya History and Religion.* Civilization of the American Indian Series 99. Norman: University of Oklahoma Press.

Thurneisser zum Thurn, Leonard

1574   *Quinta Essentia.* Leipzig.

Tomaso, Emmanuelle di, Massimillano Beltramo, and Daniele Piomelli

1996   Brain Cannabinoids in Chocolate. *Nature* 382 (6593): 677–78.

Townsend, Richard

1992   *The Aztecs.* London: Thames and Hudson.

Tozzer, Alfred M.

1907   *A Comparative Study of the Mayas and the Lacandones.* New York: Macmillan Company for the Archaeological Institute of America.

Tulley, Stephen E.

2000   Making Chocolate, Spending Pesos, Consuming Oaxaca:

Commercializing a "Traditional" Food Industry in Southern Mexico. Paper presented at the annual meeting of the Society for Applied Anthropology, San Francisco, March 24.

VanKirk, Jacques, and Parney Bassett-VanKirk

1996   *Remarkable Remains of the Ancient Peoples of Guatemala.* Norman: University of Oklahoma Press.

Von Winning, Hasso

1985   *Two Maya Monuments in Yucatan: The Palace of the Stuccoes at Acanceh and the Temple of the Owls at Chichén Itzá.* Frederick Webb Hodge Anniversary Publication Fund Series 12. Los Angeles, CA: Southwest Museum.

Waizel Bucay, José, and María Luisa Torres-Cabrera

2002   Uso tradicional e investigación científica de *Talauma mexicana* (D.C.) Don, "Yolloxochitl o Flor del Corazón"

(Magnoliaceae). *Revista Mexicana de Cardiologia* 13 (1): 31–38.

Whittington, E. Michael, ed.

2001   *The Sport of Life and Death: The Mesoamerican Ballgame.* London: Thames and Hudson.

Willard, Theodore A.

1926   *The City of the Sacred Well.* New York: Century.

Würsch, Pierre, and Paul-Andre Finot

1999   Carbohydrate and Protein. In Knight, *Chocolate and Cocoa,* 105–15.

Yoon, Carol Kaesuk

1998   Chocoholics Take Note: Beloved Bean in Peril. *New York Times,* May 4.

Young, Allen M.

1994   *The Chocolate Tree: A Natural History of Cacao.* Washington, DC: Smithsonian Institution Press.

illustration credits

~~~~~~~~~~~~

Images not credited are courtesy of Nettie Lee Benson Latin American Collection, University of Texas Libraries, University of Texas at Austin. For those Justin Kerr photographs that lack ownership citations, there is no available information on Justin Kerr's website.

Dedication page photograph by Edwardo Sacayon, www.FLAAR.org, courtesy of Museo Popol Vuh, Universidad Francisco Marroquín, no. MPV 1425.

introduction

I.1 Photograph by Edwardo Sacayon, www.FLAAR.org, courtesy of Museo Popol Vuh, Universidad Francisco Marroquín, private collection.

I.2 Photograph © George O. Jackson Jr.

1 chocolate and the supernatural realm

1.1 Photograph by Edwardo Sacayon, www.FLAAR.org, courtesy of Museo Popol Vuh, Universidad Francisco Marroquín, no. MPV 1575.

1.2 Photograph by Edwardo Sacayon, www.FLAAR.org, courtesy of Museo Popol Vuh, Universidad Francisco Marroquín, no. MPV 0282.

1.3 Photograph by Edwardo Sacayon, www.FLAAR.org, courtesy of Museo Popol Vuh, Universidad Francisco Marroquín, no. MPV 1365.

1.4 Dumbarton Oaks, Pre-Columbian Collection, Washington, DC, nos. PC.B.208.S1 and PC.B208.S2.

1.5 Photograph by Edwardo Sacayon, www.FLAAR.org, courtesy of Museo Popol Vuh, Universidad Francisco Marroquín, no. MPV 0935.

1.6 Photograph by Filmteam.

1.8 Museum of Fine Arts, Houston; gift of Mrs. Harry C. Hanszen.

1.9 Rollout photograph © Justin Kerr; file no. K5185; Denver Art Museum, no. 1989.214.

1.10 Rollout photograph © Justin Kerr; file no. K4599; Princeton Art Museum.

1.11 Rollout photograph © Justin Kerr; file no. K5070.

1.12 © 2006 Harvard University, Peabody Museum of Archaeology and Ethnology, 95-42-20/C598 N34516 and 95-42-20/C597 N34516.

1.14 Composite reconstruction drawing by Sharon Edgar Greenhill © ArcheoProductions, after a field drawing by Peter Schmidt, a rubbing by Merle Green Robertson, a photo by Hasso Von Winning, and a drawing by John Held.

1.15 Rollout photograph © Justin Kerr; file no. K631.

1.16 Rubbing by Merle Greene Robertson, Pre-Columbian Art Research Institute.

1.17 © 2006 Harvard University, Peabody Museum of Archaeology and Ethnology, 10-71-20/C7410 T2756.

1.18 Akademische Druck-u. Verlagsanstalt, Graz, Austria.

1.19 Rollout photograph © Justin Kerr; file no. K6547; Museo Popol Vuh, Guatemala.

1.20 Rollout photograph © Justin Kerr; file no. K5615; Museo Popol Vuh, Guatemala.

1.21 Drawing by Patrick Gallagher (after S. Linné) in *Mexico: From the Olmecs to the Aztecs*, 5th ed., by Michael D. Coe and Rex Koontz, p. 117, fig. 81. Courtesy of Thames and Hudson, New York.

1.22 Akademische Druck-u. Verlagsanstalt, Graz, Austria.

1.25 Akademische Druck-u. Verlagsanstalt, Graz, Austria.

1.26 Photograph © Justin Kerr; file no. K1504b.

2 chocolate and ritual in mesoamerica

2.1 Photograph © George O. Jackson Jr.

2.2 Colorized photograph by T. A. Willard, 1920. Courtesy of Autry National Center, Southwest Museum, Los Angeles. Photo no. N43284.

2.3 Photograph by Grant Mitchell © ArcheoProductions.

2.4 Fototeca Fundación G&T Continental, Museo Nacional de Arqueología y Etnología de Guatemala.

2.5a Photograph by Filmteam.

2.5b Drawing by Sharon Edgar Greenhill © ArcheoProductions.

2.6 Photograph by Filmteam.

2.7 Bildarchiv Preussischer Kulturbesitz, Art Resource, New York.

2.8 Drawing by Michael Edwin Kampen, in Kampen, *The Sculptures of El Tajín, Veracruz, Mexico*, 1972, fig. 5a. Reprinted with permission of the University Press of Florida.

2.9 Nettie Lee Benson Latin American Collection, University of Texas Libraries, University of Texas at Austin.

2.10 Akademische Druck-u. Verlagsanstalt, Graz, Austria.

2.11 Photograph © George O. Jackson Jr.

2.12 Drawing by Linda Schele, © David Schele, courtesy of Foundation for the Advancement of Mesoamerican Studies, www.famsi.org.

2.13 Photograph by Edwardo Sacayon, www.FLAAR.org, courtesy of Museo Popol Vuh, Universidad Francisco Marroquín, MPV no. 1425.

2.14 Courtesy of Milwaukee Public Museum, catalogue no. 58661 19445.

2.15–2.17 Photographs © George O. Jackson Jr.

2.18 Photograph by Grant Mitchell © ArcheoProductions.

2.19 Rollout photograph © Justin Kerr; file no. K1599.

2.21 Akademische Druck-u. Verlagsanstalt, Graz, Austria.

2.22 Photograph by Judith Strupp Green.

2.23 Photograph by Sharon Edgar Greenhill © ArcheoProductions.

2.24 Photograph by Steven L. Black.

2.25 Photograph by Keith Prufer.

2.27–2.30 Photographs © George O. Jackson Jr.

3 power, wealth, and greed

3.1 Photograph by Carlos Varillas. Fundación Amparo/Museo Amparo, Puebla, Mexico, no. 52 22 MA FA 57PJ 1465.

3.2 Rollout photograph © Justin Kerr; file no. K511; Princeton Art Museum.

3.3 Drawing by Sharon Edgar Greenhill © ArcheoProductions.

3.4 Photograph by Payson D. Sheets.

3.5 Drawing by Sharon Edgar Greenhill © ArcheoProductions, after map by John B. Garver, *National Geographic*, October 1989.

3.6 Photograph by Edwardo Sacayon, www.FLAAR.org, courtesy of Museo Popol Vuh, Universidad Francisco Marroquín, private collection.

3.7 Drawing by Sharon Edgar Greenhill after drawing in situ by Saburo Sugiyama, 1984. © 1984 René Millon, in *Feathered Serpents and Flowering Trees: Reconstructing the Murals of Teotihuacán*, ed. Kathleen Berrin. Seattle: Fine Arts Museums of San Francisco, 1988.

3.8 Photograph © 2006 Bob Sacha.

3.10 Artwork by Anne Axtell Morris, Carnegie Institution of Washington.

3.11 Rollout photograph © Justin Kerr; file no. K5453.

3.12 Artwork by Heather Hurst and Leonard Ashby, courtesy of Mary Miller, Bonampak Documentation Project.

3.13 Akademische Druck-u. Verlagsanstalt, Graz, Austria.

3.14 Akademische Druck-u. Verlagsanstalt, Graz, Austria.

3.16 Photograph by Frederick J. Bove, courtesy of the Balberta Project.

4 serve up the chocolate

4.1a–d Photographs © George O. Jackson Jr.

4.1e–f Photographs by Sharon Edgar Greenhill © ArcheoProductions.

4.2 Museo de América, Madrid.

4.3 Rollout photograph © Justin Kerr; file no. K511; Princeton Art Museum.

4.4 Photographs by Grant Mitchell, © ArcheoProductions.

4.5 Photograph © Justin Kerr; file no. K5362; Duke University Museum of Art.

4.6 Rollout photograph © Justin Kerr; file no. K8552.

4.7 Rollout photograph © Justin Kerr; file no. K530.

4.8 Drawing by Sharon Edgar Greenhill © ArcheoProductions, after Yolanda Tovar, Instituto Hondur2año de Antropologia a Historia, Museo de San Pedro Sula, Honduras.

4.9 Photograph by Sharon Edgar Greenhill © ArcheoProductions, courtesy of Thomas R. Hester, director of the Colha Project.

4.10 Rollout and normal photographs © Justin Kerr; file no. K7784.

4.11 Photograph © Justin Kerr; file no. K6785; Copan, Honduras.

4.12 Rollout photograph © Justin Kerr; file no. K4976; glyph translation by Barbara MacLeod and Dorie Reents-Budet; Los Angeles County Museum, Los Angeles.

4.13a Photograph © Justin Kerr; file no. K1183; Museum of Fine Arts, Boston, image no. 1988.1169.

4.13b Photograph © Justin Kerr; file no. 635; Art Institute of Chicago.

4.13c Drawing by Sharon Edgar Greenhill © ArcheoProductions.

4.13d Akademische Druck-u. Verlagsanstalt, Graz, Austria.

4.14 Rollout photograph © Justin Kerr; file no. K1183; courtesy of Museum of Fine Arts, Boston, image no. 1988.1169.

4.15 Photograph by Grant Mitchell, © ArcheoProductions.

4.16 Photograph by Payson D. Sheets.

4.17 University of Pennsylvania Museum; image no. 153056.

4.18 Photograph © 2006 Museum of Fine Arts, Boston, image no. 1971.496.

4.19 2006 Harvard University, Peabody Museum of Archaeology and Ethnology, MSH019.11-6-20/C5666 T1521.

4.20 Photograph © Justin Kerr; file no. K5073.

4.21 Photograph © Justin Kerr; file no. K6418.

4.22 Photograph © Michel Zabé/AZA, courtesy of Museo Regional de Yucatán, CNCA-INAH.

4.23 Photograph © Justin Kerr; file no. K4976; Los Angeles County Museum.

4.24 Image courtesy of University of Pennsylvania Museum, Early Copan Acropolis Program, and Instituto Hondureño de Anthropología e Historia. Photograph by Robert Sharer.

4.25 Photograph © Justin Kerr; file no. K5357, courtesy of Duke University Museum of Art, no. 1980.5.4a.

4.26 Photograph © Justin Kerr; file no. K635; Art Institute of Chicago.

4.27 Photograph by Edwardo Sacayon, www.FLAAR.org, courtesy of Museo Popol Vuh, Universidad Francisco Marroquín, private collection.

4.28 Photographs by Edwardo Sacayon, www.FLAAR.org, courtesy of Museo Popol Vuh, Universidad Francisco Marroquín, Colección Casa Santa Domingo Hotel-Museo.

4.29–4.31 Photographs by Sharon Edgar Greenhill © ArcheoProductions.

5 The Healing Powers of chocolate

5.1 Rollout photograph © Justin Kerr; file no. K8608.

5.2 Akademische Druck-u. Verlagsanstalt, Graz, Austria.

5.3 HIP/Art Resource, New York.

5.5 Nettie Lee Benson Latin American Collection, University of Texas Libraries, University of Texas at Austin.

5.7 Rollout photograph © Justin Kerr; file no. K1890; Metropolitan Museum of Art, New York.

5.8 Photograph © Justin Kerr; file no. K1503.

5.9 Martín de la Cruz, *Badianus Manuscript (Codex Barberini, Latin 241) Vatican Library: An Aztec Herbal of 1552*, p. 182, plate 98. © 1940 Johns Hopkins Press. Reprinted with permission of Johns Hopkins University Press.

5.10 Martín de la Cruz, *Badianus Manuscript (Codex Barberini, Latin 241) Vatican Library: An Aztec Herbal of 1552*, p. 188, plate 104. © 1940 Johns Hopkins Press. Reprinted with permission of Johns Hopkins University Press.

5.11 Photograph © Justin Kerr; file no. K4892; Museo Nacional, Guatemala.

6 Balancing the Cosmos

6.1   HM525, William P. Palmer III Collection, Hudson Museum, University of Maine.

6.2   Reconstruction drawing by Simon Martin.

6.3   Drawing by Sharon Edgar Greenhill © ArcheoProductions, after field drawing by Peter Schmidt, 2003.

6.4   Courtesy Museum of New Mexico, Palace of the Governors (MNM/DCA).

6.5   Photograph © George O. Jackson Jr.

6.6   Rollout photograph © Justin Kerr; file no. K1288.

6.7   Photograph by Allen M. Young.

6.8   Photograph © Justin Kerr; file no. K6312; Library of Congress, Jay Kislak Collection.

6.9   Rollout photograph © Justin Kerr; file no. K5369; Mint Museum of Art, Charlotte, NC, Museum no. 81.204.7.

6.10 *Cacao in the Brazilian Atlantic Forest with Pink-Legged Graveteiro*. Illustration © Michael Rothman.

6.11 Photograph © Justin Kerr; file no. K8422a.

6.12 Photograph by Grant Mitchell © ArcheoProductions.

6.13 Indianapolis Museum of Art; gift of Bonnie and David Ross.

index

NOTE: *Page numbers in italics indicate illustrations.*

flor de cacao (*Quararibea funebris*), 108, 141–42

Florentine Codex, 141

foam, 58, 79, 108, *109*, 111, 115, 128

foods, 5, 18, *122*; first, 9, 12; ritual, 6, 54, 57–58, 70, 73–76, 79, 148

forastero variety, 5, 163

Four Dog: as God L, 88

funerals, 4; offerings at, 70, *72*

gardens, 25, 80, 82–83, *140*

gifts, 66, 118

global warming, 166–67, 174n32

glyphs, 6; cacao, 78, 97, *112–13*, *120–21*, 171n21; on ceramics, *118–19*, *122–23*, *125–26*, *128–29*; chocolate "recipes" in, 111; signature, *130*

goddesses. *See* deities *and by name*

God L, 52, 55, 77, 79, 80, 88, 89, *90–91*, 172n5

god pots, *57–58*

gods. *See* deities *and by name*

gourds, 111

grass: as foaming agent, 58

graveteiro, pink-legged, *162*

Green and Black's, *167*, 169

Guanaja, 89

Guatemala, 3, 12, 48, 58, 66, 80; ceramics from, *20*, *46*, 125, *126*, *128*, *129*, *132*, *133*; kakaw serving in, *67–68*; trade with, 85, 89. *See also various regions, sites, and towns*

Guerrero, *41*, 80

hallucinogens, 148–49

harvests, 42, 58

heart flower (*Talauma mexicana*), 108, 146–47

hearts, 69; cacao pods as, 4, 48–49

Hernández, Francisco, 141

Hero Twins, *20*, *22*, 28, 29, *34*, 122

Hershey Chocolate Company, 144; chemical testing by, 70, 115, 125

hieroglyphs. *See* glyphs

Historia de las Plantas de la Nueva España (Hernández), 141

Honduras, 3, 80, 93, 102; vessels from, *114–15*, *122–23*, 125. *See also various regions and sites*

households, 82–83

Hoy Uk Kían, 148

Huaxtepec (Oaxtepec), 140

Hunahpú, 28, *34*

iguanas: as offerings, 59

Imix, 154

imix-ché, 154, 158, 171n22

incensarios. *See* censers

Indonesia, 165

insects, 137; as pollinators, 158–60

irrigation systems, 80, 164

Itzamna, 35, 37, 38, 42, 111, 122, 155, *156*

Ivory Coast, 165

IxChel, 35, *36*

Izapa, 154

jaguars, 4, *162*; as guardian, 44–47

Jesus: as god of wet season, 55

jimsonweed (*Datura stramonium*), 149

kakaw: serving, 67–68

K'awil, 27, 35, 42, 43, 77, *78*

Kuna, 151

Lacandon Chol Maya, 55, 57, 108, 111

Lady Thirteen Serpent, 64, *65*

Landa, Diego de: observations of, 58–59, 66–67, 80, 82, 172n36

Land of the Dead: cacao tree and, 25

Libellus de Medicinalibus Indorum Herbis, 146

lineages: trees as, 25, 27–28

Lopez de Cogolludo, Diego, 52

Lord Eight Deer, 64, *65*

Lords of the Underworld, 28

madre de cacao (*Gliricidia sepium*), 22, 157–58

Madrid Codex, 28, 35, 58; baptisms in, 66–67; gods in, *31*, *36*, 38

maize, 41, 55, 106, 171n10; rituals with, 58–63

maize god, 28, *34*, 56

Mam (MaXimón) 52, 54, 55

mamey tree (*Calocarpum mammosum*), 108

marble vases, *122–23*

Margarita tomb, 115

marijuana, 149

markets, 98, 102; world, 164–65

marriages, 4, 64, *65–66*

MaXimón (Mam), 52, 54, 55

Maya, 4, 5, 6, 18, 21, 25, 41, 77, 83, 94, 130, 143, 151, 154, 165; creation, 9–10, 12, 171n10, 171n22; deities, *32–33*, 35–39, 88; ruling dynasties, 27–28; sacrifice symbolism, 48–49; Underworld, 135–36; vessel forms, *114–15*; World Tree, *22–23*. *See also various groups and sites*

Maya Mountains, 42

Mayapan, 82, 93

medicine: Aztec, 135, 136–37, 139–40, 141–43; Spanish, 137–38

merchant gods: Mayan, 54, 55, 88, 89, *90–91*, 92; Aztec, 98, *99*

merchants, 83, 88, 98, 171n4

midges: as pollinators, 158–60

Milky Way, 154, 173n1

Mixtecs, 4, 15, 18, 52, 53, 64, *65*, 108, 124

Moctezuma, 77, 99, 111, 140, 146

mole, 73, 74, 125, *126*, *127*

molonillo, 108, *133*

money: cacao seeds as, 66, 101–2

monkeys, 4, 45, *20–22*, *160*, *161*, *162*

about the Authors

~~~~~~~~~~~~~~~

meredith preiss holds a BA in anthropology from California State University–Sonoma (1978) and an MA in anthropology with a specialization in Mayan archaeology from the University of Texas at San Antonio (1986). She is currently a research fellow at the Texas Archaeological Research Laboratory at the University of Texas at Austin. For over twenty years, she has participated in excavation, field camp management, artifact analysis, academic writing and speaking, and other research interests with a variety of academic and commercial partners. Her company, ArcheoProductions, Inc. (www.archeoproductions.com), develops and produces anthropology-related educational and entertainment projects in a variety of media. In 2005, it produced the documentary film *Chocolate: Pathway to the Gods*. Meredith is also president of the Cynthia and George Mitchell Foundation, which focuses on global sustainability issues.

sharon greenhill has more than twenty years of professional experience in the fields of architecture, museum design, and historic preservation, including nearly a decade as director of planning for Laguna Gloria Art Museum's building project and vice-chair on the Austin Historic Landmark Commission. Author of *Historic Austin*, she has consulted nationwide on museum design and preservation projects. Holding MSCRP and MArchS degrees from the University of Texas School of Architecture, she presently focuses on sixteenth-century, pre-Columbian, and contact period architecture, iconography, and culture. She participates annually in conferences on Mixtec codices and Maya vases and codices, while archiving digital images of Mesoamerican material. She is a long-time consultant to ArcheoProductions, Inc., and was coproducer of the film *Chocolate: Pathway to the Gods*.

Library of Congress Cataloging-in-Publication Data

Dreiss, Meredith L.
  Chocolate : pathway to the gods / Meredith L. Dreiss
and Sharon Edgar Greenhill.
    p. cm.
  Includes bibliographical references and index.
  ISBN 978-0-8165-2464-8 (hardcover : alk. paper)
  1. Chocolate—History. 2. Chocolate—Central
America—History. 3. Chocolate—Mexico—History.
I. Greenhill, Sharon. II. Title.
TX817.C4D74   2008
641.6'37409—dc22   2008018868

DATE DUE

MAR 05 2009			
APR 2 6 2016			